ECONOMIC ISSUES, PROBLEMS AND PERSPECTIVES SERIES

NAFTA STOCK MARKETS: DYNAMIC RETURN AND VOLATILITY LINKAGES

ECONOMIC ISSUES, PROBLEMS AND PERSPECTIVES SERIES

Trust, Globalisation and Market Expansion
Jacques-Marie Aurifeille, Christopher Medlin, and Clem Tisdell
2009. ISBN: 978-1-60741-812-2

TARP in the Crosshairs: Accountability in the Troubled Asset Relief Program
Paul W. O'Byrne (Editor)
2009. ISBN: 978-1-60741-807-8

TARP in the Crosshairs: Accountability in the Troubled Asset Relief Program
Paul W. O'Byrne (Editor)
2009. ISBN: 978-1-60876-705-2 *(Online book)*

Government Interventions in Economic Emergencies
Pablo Sastre (Editor)
2010. ISBN: 978-1-60741-356-1

NAFTA Stock Markets: Dynamic Return and Volatility Linkages
Giorgio Canarella, Stephen M. Miller and Stephen K. Pollard
2010. ISBN: 978-1-60876-498-3

ECONOMIC ISSUES, PROBLEMS AND PERSPECTIVES SERIES

NAFTA STOCK MARKETS: DYNAMIC RETURN AND VOLATILITY LINKAGES

GIORGIO CANARELLA,
STEPHEN M. MILLER
AND
STEPHEN K. POLLARD

Nova Science Publishers, Inc.
New York

For permission to use material from this book please contact us:
Telephone 631-231-7269; Fax 631-231-8175
Web Site: http://www.novapublishers.com

LIBRARY OF CONGRESS CATALOGING-IN-PUBLICATION DATA
Available upon request
ISBN: 978-1-60876-498-3

Published by Nova Science Publishers, Inc. ✦ New York

CONTENTS

ABSTRACT

This research explores the dynamic linkages that portray different facets of the joint probability distribution of stock market returns in the North American Free Trade Area (NAFTA) – Canada, Mexico, and the US. Our examination of interactions of the NAFTA stock markets considers three issues. First, we examine the long-run relationship between the three markets, using cointegration techniques. Second, we evaluate the dynamic relationships between the three markets, using impulse-response analysis. Finally, we explore the volatility transmission process between the three markets, using a multivariate generalized autoregressive conditional heteroskedasticity model. Our results exhibit significant volatility transmission between the second moments of the NAFTA stock markets, albeit not homogenous. The magnitude and trend of the conditional correlations indicate that in the last few years, Mexico's stock market exhibited a tendency toward increased integration with the US market. Finally, we do note that evidence exists that the Peso and Asian financial crises as well as the stock-market crash in the US affect the return and volatility time-series relationships.

Keywords: NAFTA stock markets, cointegration, impulse response, volatility transmission

JEL Code: G10, C30, C50

Chapter 1

INTRODUCTION

Over the past twenty years, international equity markets grew increasingly interdependent (e.g., Jeon and Chiang, 1991; Kasa, 1992; Rangvid, 2001). Regional and global cooperation, deregulation, and market liberalization contributed to international financial integration and interdependence (Fraser and Oyefeso, 2005; Aggarwal and Kyaw, 2005). Advances in computer technology and information processing also reduced the segmentation of domestic equity markets and increased their ability to react promptly to news originating in the rest of the world. Finally, new, common trading blocs, such as the European Union (EU), the Association of Southeast Asian Nations (ASEAN), the Southern Common Market (MERCOSUR), and the North American Free Trade Agreement (NAFTA), as well as new, integrated economic systems such as the European Monetary Union (EMU) enhanced the interdependence between national equity markets of those member states (Chen, Firth, and Rui, 2002).

The growth and reach of international trade and finance reveal two important stylized facts. First, although the growth in trade preceded the growth of finance, the growth and spread of international finance eventually surpassed that of trade (Krugman and Obstfeld, 2009; Feenstra and Taylor, 2008). Second, much trade growth reflected the creation of regional trade groups (e.g., ASEAN, MERCOSUR, EU, and NAFTA). Feenstra and Taylor (2008) show that intraregional trade dominates interregional trade, which fostered research dedicated to regional financial markets. Not surprisingly, much recent research examines international financial markets with a regional emphasis (e.g., Asian and Latin American financial markets in emerging markets and the EU and NAFTA in developed countries).

The changing patterns of international trade precipitated larger capital flows across markets, further enhancing the integration and globalization process. MacDermott (2007) concludes that NAFTA increased foreign direct investment (FDI) flows into the US by approximately 0.96 percent, while flows into Mexico and Canada rose by 1.73 and 1.54 percent. Globerman and Shapiro (1999) and Karp and Sanchez (2000) report similar, but smaller, country-specific results. The rapid growth of financial-market integration portends obvious implications for international portfolio diversification, international asset pricing, hedging strategies, and regulatory policy.[1]

Previous research largely conducted investigations of international equity-market linkages along two lines. First, researchers consider whether cointegration (Engle and Granger, 1987; Johansen 1988, 1991, 1995; Johansen and Juselius, 1990) exists among international equity markets. Evidence of cointegration indicates that stock markets follow the same long-run stochastic trend, implying that any diversification gains across international markets only occurs at short-run horizons when markets can temporarily diverge from their long-run path.[2]

The efficient-market hypothesis in its strong form argues that a stock's price incorporates all the known, relevant information about the company. Thus, only "news" about that company moves this period's stock price. Granger (1992) argued "... for the same reason one would not expect a pair of stock prices to be cointegrated, as this would contradict the efficient market hypothesis." (p. 11). Consider two regional stock markets that make a market in the same firm. The law of one price implies the same price in the two markets, ignoring transactions costs and making any needed exchange rate adjustment. Thus, cointegration between the two prices should exist. The cointegration studies that we cite consider market indices rather than individual stock prices. As a consequence, if countries contain similar industry mixes, then cointegration between stock market indices in different countries may make sense.

Second, researchers explore the time-series properties of the conditional second moments of the returns, which prove important in many financial applications. Engle (1982) set in motion the extension of traditional time-series

---

[1] For example, the current global financial crisis highlights the lack of supernational regulation, which will likely change in the near future.

[2] Numerous studies exist that examine stock market integration using cointegration techniques. An abbreviated list includes the following: Taylor and Tonks (1989), Eun and Shim (1989) Jeon and Chiang (1991), Becker et al. (1995), Kasa (1992), Arshanapalli and Doukas (1993), Chorhay et al. (1993), Blackman et al. (1994), Arshanapalli et al. (1997), Richards (1995), Choudhry (1996), Masih and Masih (1997), Roca (1999), Ghosh et al. (1999), Pan et al. (1999), Chang (2001), Ostermark (2001), Chen et al. (2002), Manning (2002), Sharma and Wongbangpo (2002), Aggarwal and Kyaw (2005) and Fraser and Oyefeso (2005).

tools such as autoregressive moving average (ARMA) models for the conditional mean to essentially analogous models for the conditional variance. Autoregressive conditional heteroskedasticity (ARCH) models now commonly capture the volatility dynamics of financial time series.[3]

The empirical success of ARCH models in fitting univariate time series motivated many researchers to extend these models into multivariate contexts. That financial volatilities move together over time, across assets and markets is a stylized fact. Multivariate modeling should lead to more relevant empirical models and deeper insights into financial markets than working with separate univariate models. The motivation for multivariate generalized autoregressive conditional heteroskedasticity (GARCH) models relies on the fact that international stock prices react, at least in part, to the same information, and consequently, exhibit nonzero covariances, conditional on the information set available. In finance, multivariate GARCH modeling opens the door to better decision tools in various areas such as asset pricing, portfolio selection, hedging, and Value-at-Risk forecasts. Although a huge literature exists on univariate models for volatility dynamics, asymmetry, and fat-tails, much fewer studies concentrate on their multivariate extensions.

Cointegration analysis only provides a binary outcome: markets are either integrated or segmented. Bekaert and Harvey (1995) emphasize, however, that market integration involves a complex dynamic process. Conditional correlations, rather than cointegration, may more adequately and completely describe the process. The multivariate GARCH framework allows the modeling of the conditional correlations and covariances, analyzing the multilateral feedback among markets, and examining the dynamic links between market information and volatility. Further, unlike the cointegration approach, which does not go beyond linkages between the first moments, the multivariate GARCH approach measures the extent of market integration through both the first and the second moments of the returns in the stock exchanges.[4]

---

[3] This literature includes the ARCH and GARCH models of Engle (1982) and Bollerslev (1987) and their various nonlinear generalizations, such as nonlinear GARCH models of Bera and Higgins (1992), EGARCH models of Nelson (1991), threshold GARCH models of Glosten et al. (1993), quadratic GARCH models of Sentana (1995), threshold ARCH models of Zakoian (1994), and so on. Bollerslev et al. (1992), Bera and Higgins (1993), Bollerslev et al. (1994) survey the literature on ARCH models.

[4] Important examples of multivariate volatility models include diagonal multivariate and VECH-representation GARCH models of Bollerslev et al. (1988), the constant-correlation multivariate GARCH (CC-MGARCH) models of Bollerslev (1990), the BEKK (named after Baba, Engle, Kraft and Kroner) models of Engle and Kroner (1995), and the dynamic conditional correlation models of Engle (2002) and Tse and Tsui (2002). Several applications of multivariate (mostly bivariate) GARCH models to the investigation of linkages between stock markets exist. They

This research explores the dynamic linkages that portray different facets of the joint probability distributions of stock market returns in NAFTA (i.e., Canada, Mexico, and the US). Our examination of interactions of the NAFTA stock markets considers three issues. First, we examine the long-run relationship between the three markets, using the cointegration techniques of Johansen and Juselius (1990). Second, we evaluate the dynamic relationships between the three markets, using impulse-response analysis. Finally, we explore the volatility transmission process between the three markets, using a variety of multivariate GARCH models. Further, the extant literature offers two approaches to multivariate GARCH models. One, researchers employ models that directly specify the structure of the conditional covariance matrix, such as the VECH model of Bollerslev et al. (1988) and the BEKK model of Engle and Kroner (1995). Two, researchers employ models that specify the conditional correlations, such as the constant conditional correlation (CCC) model of Bollerslev (1990) and the dynamic-conditional-correlation (DCC) model of Engle (2002). Bauwens, et al. (2006) provide an overview of the various issues.

Several findings emerge. First, significant volatility transmission exists between the second moments of the NAFTA stock markets, albeit not homogenous. Second, the magnitude and trend of the conditional correlations indicate that in the last few years, the Mexican stock market exhibited a tendency toward increased integration with the US market. Finally, evidence emerges that the Peso and Asian financial crises as well as the stock-market crash in the US affect the return and volatility time-series relationships.

The rest of the work unfolds as follows. Chapter 2 briefly reviews the extant literature on NAFTA stock markets. Chapter 3 contains a concise discussion of the data used in our analysis. Chapter 4 explores the long-run dynamics of the returns in the North American markets, using the cointegration tests of Johansen and Juselius (1990). The Johansen and Juselius (1990) conventional cointegration methods cannot provide an understanding of the dynamics of the relationship between the three markets. We assess the expanding relationships between the North American markets, using recursive cointegration techniques proposed by Hansen and Johansen (1993) and Rangvid (2001). Structural breaks can also induce changes in the long-run relationships. To avoid weak inferences, we conduct further tests by using advanced time-series techniques such as the Zivot

include, among others, Hamao et al. (1990), King and Wadhwani (1990), Theodosiou and Lee (1993), Karolyi (1995), Koutmos (1996), Lin et al. (1994), Engle and Susmel (1993), Koutmos and Booth (1995), Booth et al. (1997), Worthington and Higgs (2004), In et al. (2001), Liu et al. (1996), Liu et al. (1998), Ang and Bekaert (2002), Brooks and Ragunathan (2003), Wang et al. (2004), and Cotter (2004).

and Andrews (1992) unit-root tests and the Gregory and Hansen (1996) cointegration tests. Chapter 5 examines the short-run linkages, using the generalized impulse-response analysis by Pesaran and Shin (1998).[5] As previously noted, however, integration analysis based upon the cointegration methodology assesses the linkages between the NAFTA stock markets based upon the first unconditional moments of the returns series. This paper's principal contribution assesses the NAFTA stock market linkages, focusing on the second moments with multivariate GARCH approaches. Chapter 6 introduces the framework of multivariate GARCH used in this paper. Following the work of Golsten et al. (1993), we consider specifications that allow for leverage or asymmetric effects in the conditional innovations. Further, given the widely recognized rejection of normality for GARCH models, we also consider the *t*-distribution with its thicker tails than the Gaussian distribution and estimate each specification with multivariate Gaussian and *t*-distributions. We report the results of the estimation of the various specifications of the multivariate GARCH models in Chapter 7. Finally, Chapter 8 summarizes and concludes.

[5] This methodology dominates the more traditional orthogonalized approach developed by Sims (1980), such as the Cholesky factorization, in that the impulse-response functions prove invariant to the ordering of variables in the vector autoregressive model. Dekker et al. (2001) compare the traditional approach to impulse-response functions developed by Sims (1980) to the generalized approach by Pesaran and Shin (1998) and finds that the generalized approach gives more realistic results, particularly for those markets with close geographical and economic links.

Chapter 2

EXISTING EMPIRICAL ANALYSIS OF NAFTA STOCK MARKETS

Existing empirical studies of these North American stock markets pay attention predominantly to the long-run linkages and co-movements between the three markets (e.g., Attenberry and Swanson, 1997; Ewing et al., 1999, 2001; Gilmore and McManus, 2004; Darrat and Zhong, 2005; Ciner, 2006; Ortiz et al., 2008; Aggarwal and Kyaw, 2005; and Phengpis and Swanson, 2006). Ewing et al. (1999) find no evidence of cointegration among stock market price indices in the three NAFTA countries, even after including a dummy variable to account for the implementation of NAFTA in January 1994. In a related study, Ewing et al. (2001) report no evidence of daily volatility transmission among NAFTA stock markets during the pre-NAFTA period (1992:06:02 to 1993:12:31). They do, however, detect significant volatility transmission from the US to the Canadian and Mexican stock markets, but not vice versa, during the post-NAFTA period (1994:01:03 to 1999:10:28). These two studies jointly imply that the passage of NAFTA enhanced the short-run, but not necessarily long-run, linkages among the members' stock markets. Moreover, the linkages reflect the volatility of stock market returns, the second moment, and not stock market returns, the first moment.

In contrast, other related studies report evidence of cointegration among NAFTA stock markets, especially after the passage of NAFTA. That is, long-run linkages exist between stock market returns. Darrat and Zhong (2005), using weekly data from 1989 to 1999, find no evidence of cointegration during the pre-NAFTA period, but evidence of cointegration during the post-NAFTA period. Gilmore and McManus (2004), who study only the post-NAFTA period (1994–

2002), report a cointegrating relationship based on both weekly and monthly data. These studies collectively suggest that NAFTA implementation improved equity-market integration and linkages among the member nations. Further, Atteberry and Swanson (1997) test for short- and long-run relationships among the three NAFTA stock markets for each annual sub-sample from 1985 to 1994 with daily data. The results indicate consistently strong contemporaneous determination, especially between Canada and the US, but intermittent existence of cointegrating relations from one year to the next. They suggest that the exceptionally strong statistical significance of cointegrating relations in 1993 and 1994 potentially reflect economic uncertainty affecting investors' perceptions of the effects of NAFTA passage on domestic economies similar to the effect of the US stock market crash of 1987.

Phengpis and Swanson (2006) conclude that the passage of NAFTA probably reinforced economic interdependence among member countries, but it did not contribute to the long-run interdependence among the members' stock markets through consistent cointegrating relation(s). Cointegration, thus, appears time-varying, but statistically short lived. It emerges strongly during periods of economic uncertainty. These results support those in Ewing et al. (1999) who report no evidence of cointegration, even accounting for NAFTA passage in 1994. These results differ, however, from Darrat and Zhong (2005) and Gilmore and McManus (2004), who report evidence of cointegration during different pre-determined post-NAFTA periods. Thus, the long-run interrelationships among NAFTA stock markets may prove sample-dependent, or specifically, time-varying. Thus, proper investigation may require dynamic, rather than static, analysis such as rolling or recursive cointegration methodology.

Ciner (2006), using weekly data from January 2, 1994 to November 17, 2004, reports the results of testing for long-term linkages between the three markets before and after the stock market crash. Following Brooks and Del Negro (2004), Ciner (2006) identifies the breakpoint as March 1, 2000 and specifies the period between January 2, 1994 and February 29, 2000 as the pre-crash period and March 1, 2000 to November 17, 2004 as the post-crash period. Ciner (2006) conducts the empirical analysis separately for each sub-period as well as for the full sample and finds that the NAFTA equity markets support cointegration only in the pre-crash period. The test statistics indicate that the stable relation between the indices fell apart and no evidence exists of cointegration in the post-crash period. In fact, the evidence against cointegration in the latter part of the sample exhibits such strength that it overturns the favorable results in the full sample.

Ortiz et al. (2008), using daily data from August 15, 1984 to December 22, 2005, analyze returns and volatility dynamics among the NAFTA capital markets using a vector error-correction (VEC) model, which integrates GARCH effects in a process of dynamic conditional correlations. Their findings suggest that at least one long-run statistically significant equilibrium relationship exists between returns observed in the NAFTA capital markets. This evidence matches that in Darrat and Zhong (2005) and Gilmore and McManus (2004). Their findings also suggest that (a) the US market influences the short-run dynamics of the Canadian and Mexican markets; (b) the Canadian market influences the short-run dynamics of the US and Mexican markets; and (c) the Mexican market does not influence the short-run dynamics of the other two markets. Furthermore, the results from the DCC model suggest that (a) the Canadian market influences volatility in the Mexican market, but the Mexican market does not influence volatility in the Canadian market; and (b) the US market influences volatility in the Mexican and Canadian markets and the Mexican market, but not the Canadian market, affects the volatility in the US market. These results confirm the dominant role of the US market in the North American area and suggest that these three markets do not reflect full integration.

With the exception of Ortiz et al. (2008), the investigation of volatility transmission between the three North American markets rarely appears in the literature. Karolyi (1995) examines the short-run dynamics of returns and volatility for stocks traded on the New York and Toronto stock exchanges within a bivariate GARCH structure and finds that inferences about the magnitude and persistence of return innovations that originate in either market and that transmit to the other market depend importantly on how researchers model the cross-market dynamics in volatility. Adler and Qi (2003) investigate the process of integration between the Mexican and North American equity markets between 1991 and 2002, using a model that combines the domestic and international versions of capital asset pricing model.

The extent of interdependence between the Canadian, Mexican, and US stock markets directly affects North American capital integration. That is, did the enactment of NAFTA lead to more integrated North American capital markets? NAFTA greatly reduced or eliminated tariffs and other trade barriers on products and services of the three North American nations.[1] In addition, NAFTA promoted capital flows across borders by relaxing restrictions on cross-country investment and ownership of foreign stocks. The integration of capital markets between the three North American countries in the post NAFTA period affects investors, corporate managers, and policy makers. Integrated capital markets imply reduced long-term diversification benefits available to market participants, where short-

[1] Although implemented on January 1, 1994, it did not exert full force until 2000.

term correlations overstate the benefits of diversification for long-term investors. Hedging strategies depend on relatively isolated, idiosyncratic shocks to stock markets. If shocks to returns and volatilities in the US travel quickly across the Canadian and Mexican borders, then the benefits of diversification are bounded and significantly diluted.

Chen and Zhang (1997) find that countries with strong economic ties (i.e., greater bilateral trade) exhibit co-movement of financial markets. As noted, intraregional trade dominated interregional trade, where NAFTA is no exception. Intraregional trade increased dramatically among the three NAFTA nations. Between 1993 and 2004, total trade between the United States and its NAFTA partners increased 129.3 percent (110.1 percent with Canada and 100.9 percent with Mexico); yet total trade between the United States and non-NAFTA partners increased 123.8 percent in the same period.[2] Hufbauer and Schott (2005) argue that overall, NAFTA did not cause trade diversion, aside from a few select industries such as textiles and apparel, where the rules of origin negotiated in the agreement specifically made US firms prefer Mexican manufacturers. NAFTA intensified the already strong trade ties between Mexico and the US and Canada (Daniels and Vanhoose, 2004). For example, Canada's trade shares of both exports and imports with respect to Mexico doubled between 1994 and 2006. The US's trade shares with respect to Mexico increased by approximately 35 percent. Mexico also dramatically increased its trade shares over the same time period with Canada, but less so with respect to the US. Canada and the US were major trading partners before and after NAFTA.

[2] For details, see http://www.census.gov/foreign-trade/balance/c2010.html and http://www.ic.gc.ca/epic/site/tdo-dcd.nsf/en/Home

Chapter 3

DATA AND DESCRIPTIVE STATISTICS

We employ daily closing price indices for the stock markets in Canada, Mexico, and the US (i.e., the S&P TSX Composite Index in Canada, the IPC index in Mexico, and the S&P500 index in the US, respectively).[1] The series come from Commodities Systems Inc. Following the common practice, we denominate all indices in local currency. The data cover the period January 2, 1992 to December 31, 2007. We remove information from the other two markets, when the other market does not open. This yields a total of 3,790 observations for each series over 16 years. This time span involves periods of significant market

[1] The Indice de Precios y Cotizaciones (IPC) includes 35 stocks that trade on the Mexico Stock Exchange (Bolsa Mexicana de Valores). The IPC, the main index of stock market performance, expresses market yield based on the price variations from a balanced, weighted, and representative sample of the total stock certificates quoted on the Mexico Stock Exchange. Analysts update the sample on a yearly basis and include approximately 35 issuers from different sectors of the economy. Applied in its current structure since 1978, the IPC accurately expresses the status of the stock exchange market and constitutes a highly reliable index. The IPC reflects market capitalization. That is, the IPC weights the participation of each of the issuers that constitute the sample, based on the market value of the outstanding shares. The Mexico Stock Exchange defines the calculation and adjustment of rights method. The IPC updates automatically in real time, as a consequence of the execution of registered trades of the stock certificates included in the sample during the capital market auction session. The S&P TSX Composite Index currently includes a list of the largest companies on the Toronto Stock Exchange as measured by market capitalization. The Toronto Stock Exchange listed companies in this index comprise about 71 percent of market capitalization for all Canadian-based companies listed on the TSX. The S&P 500 contains the stocks of 500 large capitalization corporations, mostly US. The index proves the most notable of the many indices owned and maintained by Standard & Poor's, a division of McGraw-Hill. The S&P 500 index forms part of the broader S&P 1500 and S&P Global 1200 stock market indices. Only the stock of large publicly held companies that trade on the two largest US stock markets, the New York Stock Exchange, and Nasdaq appear in the index.

volatility in all three markets, as well as periods of relative calm. The daily returns equal the first difference of logarithmic prices multiplied by 100:

a) S&P500

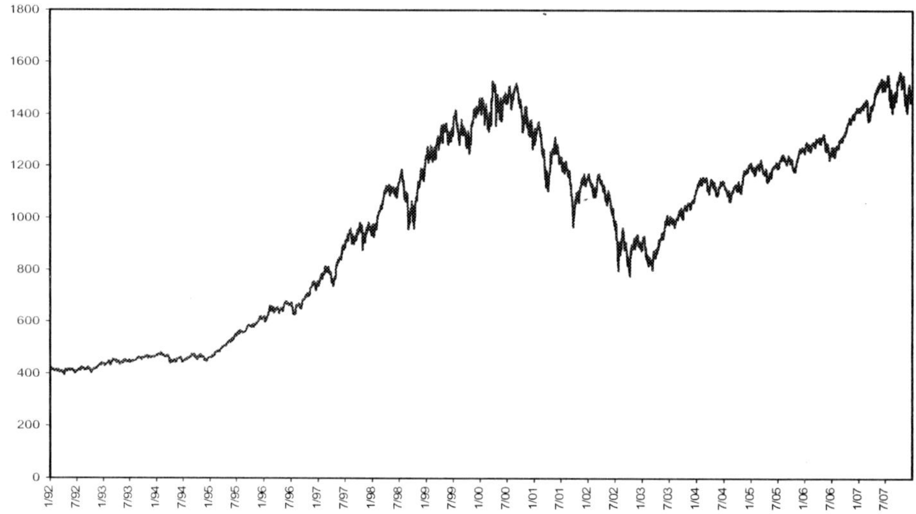

b) IPC

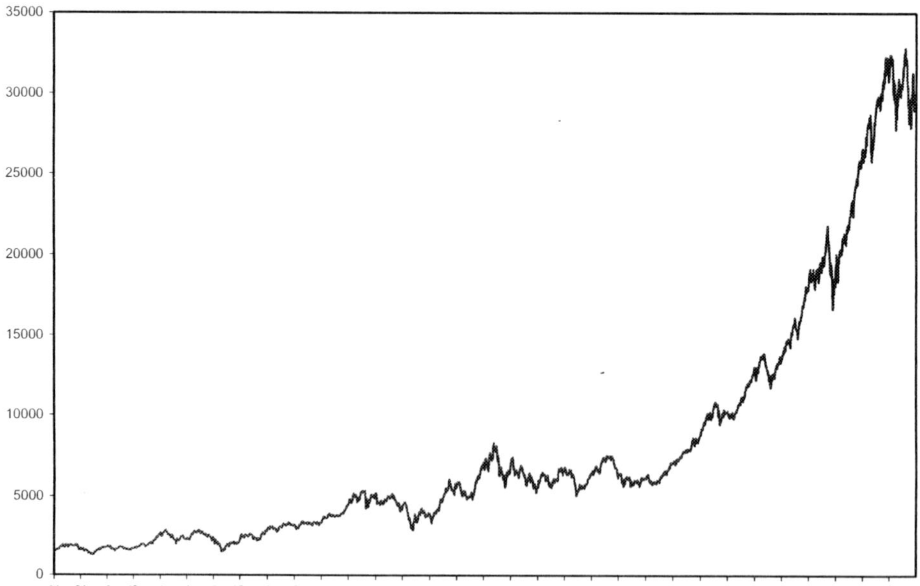

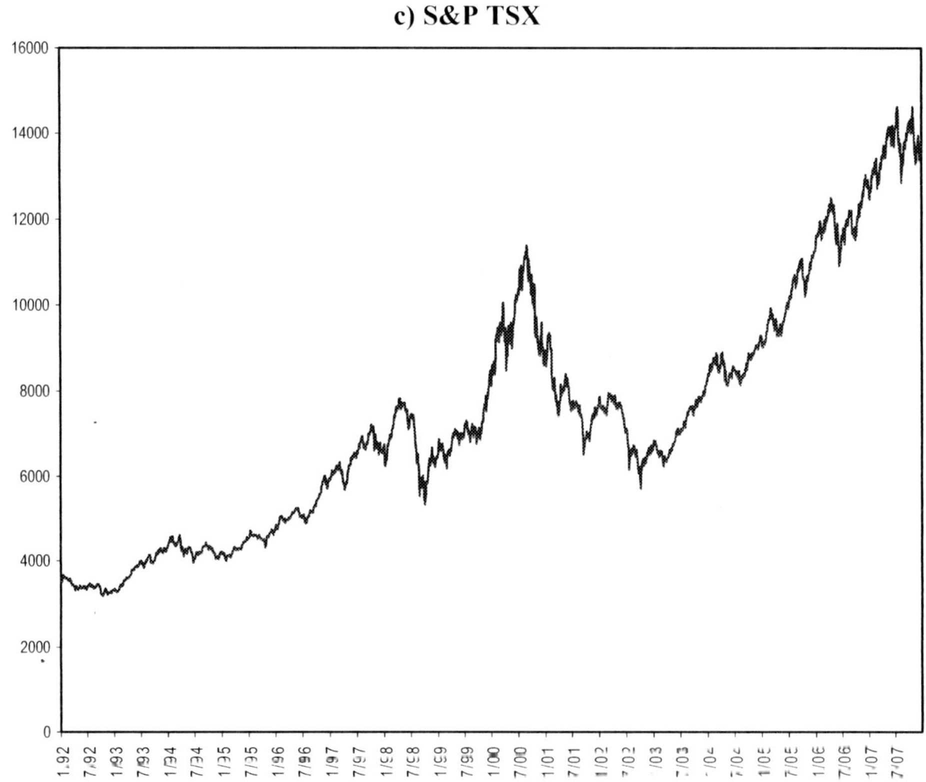

Figure 3.1. Stock Price Indices 1992-2007.

Figure 3.1 plots the three indices. Visual inspection suggests that the stock market crash of 2001 only affected the US and Canadian markets. Figure 3.2 plots the returns time series. Visual inspection suggests that the three series of returns exhibit stationarity around the mean. Moreover, a strong tendency for the volatility of the stock index returns to cluster exists. That is, large (small) returns generally follow large (small) returns, suggesting that volatility changes over time. Volatility clustering, a characteristic feature found in many asset returns, continues to receive continual documentation since the initial observation of Mandelbrot (1963) and Fama (1965).

a) S&P 500

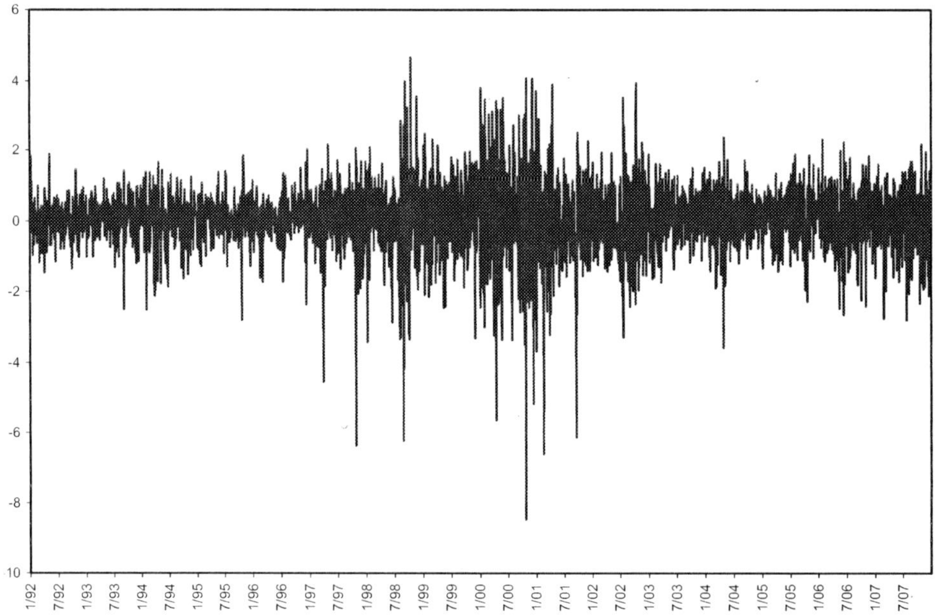
6
4
2
0
-2
-4
-6
-8
-10
1/92
7/92
1/93
7/93
1/94
7/94
1/95
7/95
1/96
7/96
1/97
7/97
1/98
7/98
1/99
7/99
1/00
7/00
1/01
7/01
1/02
7/02
1/03
7/03
1/04
7/04
1/05
7/05
1/06
7/06
1/07
7/07

b) IPC

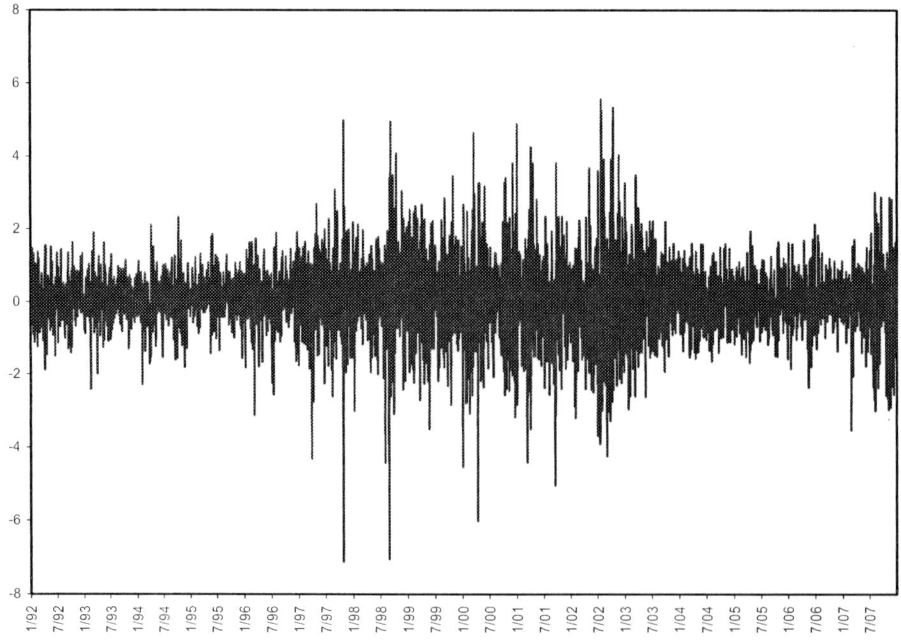
8
6
4
2
0
-2
-4
-6
-8
1/92
7/92
1/93
7/93
1/94
7/94
1/95
7/95
1/96
7/96
1/97
7/97
1/98
7/98
1/99
7/99
1/00
7/00
1/01
7/01
1/02
7/02
1/03
7/03
1/04
7/04
1/05
7/05
1/06
7/06
1/07
7/07

c) S&P TSX

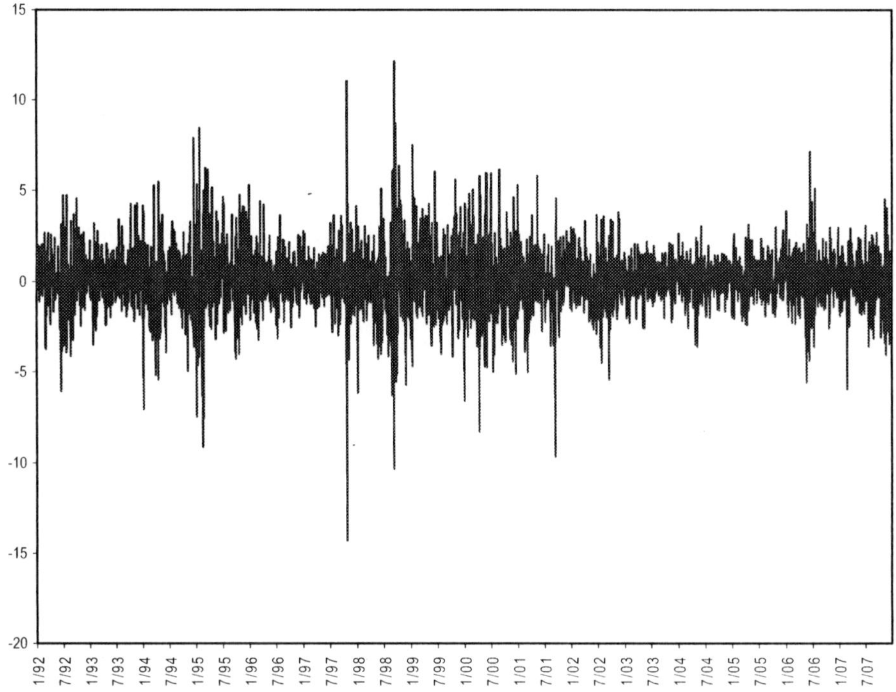

Figure 3.2. Stock Price Returns 1992-2007.

Table 3.1 reports descriptive statistics of the returns series, detailing the first four sample moments of each series. The summary statistics offer several preliminary insights into the data. The performance of the three equity markets displays positive returns, on average. The risk-return pattern appears consistent with the implications of finance theory. Mexico achieved the highest average return (0.079 per cent), followed by Canada (0.036 per cent), and then the US (0.033). For sample standard deviations, Mexico experienced a higher unconditional volatility (1.672) compared to the US (1.034 per cent) and Canada (0.923).

All three markets possess negative skewness, indicating that large negative shocks occur more frequently than large positive shocks. The IPC, however, illustrates only slight negative skewness, while the S&P TSX shows heavy negative skewness. All returns series display a measure of kurtosis than exceeds three and fail the Jarque-Bera test of normality. That is, all three series exhibit heavy tails and positive excess kurtosis. Thus, the distributional properties of the returns series generally appear non-normal.

In all cases, the p-values for the Jarque-Bera statistic reject the null hypothesis of normality at the 1-percent level. We also check the normality assumption with the multivariate test of Doornik and Hansen (1994), based on Shenton and Bowman (1977). For each of the n series, we transform the measure of skewness, $\sqrt{b_{1j}}$ for $j = 1, \ldots, n$, to a standard normal Z_{1j} as in D'Agostino (1970), while we transform the measure of kurtosis, b_{2j}, from a gamma to a chi-square distribution and then to a standard normal Z_{2j} using the Wilson and Hilferty (1931) cubed-root transformation.

Doornik and Hansen (1994) propose the following test statistic:

$$E_p = Z_1'Z_1 + Z_2'Z_2, \tag{3.1}$$

where $Z_1 = (Z_{11},\ldots Z_{1j},\ldots Z_{1n})'$ and $Z_2 = (Z_{21},\ldots Z_{2j},\ldots Z_{2n})'$. Under the null hypothesis of normality, the test statistic is approximately distributed as chi-square with $2n$ degrees of freedom. The Doornik-Hansen test statistic equals 4,340.23, which is significant at the 1-percent level. This indicates that a significant departure from normality in the joint returns distribution of the returns exists.

Table 3.1. Summary Statistics of the Return Series

	Canada	**Mexico**	**US**
Mean	0.036319	0.079641	0.033206
Median	0.064505	0.077828	0.055146
Maximum	4.683352	12.15364	5.573247
Minimum	-8.465626	-14.31446	-7.113885
Std. Dev.	0.923267	1.672076	1.034008
Skewness	-0.717208	-0.090087	-0.152942
Kurtosis	9.682723	8.433533	6.915857
Jarque-Bera	7375.34	4666.11	2435.62

Note: Daily returns equal the first difference of logarithmic prices in percent.

Table 3.2. Ljung-Box Statistics Applied to Returns and Squared Returns

	Returns		
	Canada	**Mexico**	**US**
LB-Q(6)	37.725	38.566	20.900
LB-Q(12)	56.545	54.637	41.278
LB-Q(18)	64.074	67.999	44.632
LB-Q(24)	68.701	70..072	52.736
	Squared Returns		
	Canada	**Mexico**	**US**
LB-Q^2(6)	465.92	549.81	724.73
LB-Q^2(12)	719.16	709.21	1105.1
LB-Q^2(18)	913.47	864.11	1453.6
LB-Q^2(24)	1114.1	936.38	1731.8

Note: LB-Q and LB-Q^2 equal the Ljung-Box statistics for the returns and squared returns, respectively. Number of lags appears in parentheses.

We test for the presence of intertemporal dependencies in the returns and squared returns using the Ljung-Box portmanteau test. Table 3.2 summarizes the results. The Ljung-Box (LB) statistic tests the hypothesis that autocorrelations up to the nth lag are jointly statistically significant. The calculated LB statistics at six, twelve, eighteen, and twenty-four lags, given by LB-Q(6), LB-Q(12), LB-Q(18), and LB-Q(24), firmly reject the hypothesis of linear independence at the 1-percent level in each of the three returns, implying that the conditional mean of the distribution of each return depends on past returns.

Similarly, we also firmly reject the hypothesis of independence in each of the three squared returns at the 1-percent level. The LB statistics for the squared returns at six, twelve, eighteen, and twenty-four lags, given by LB-Q^2(6), LB-Q^2(12), LB-Q^2(18), and LB-Q^2(24), exceed by several times those of the returns themselves. That is, higher-moment dependencies prove much more pronounced. Significant serial correlations in squared returns typically imply volatility clustering and time-varying variances.

Hosking (1980) derives the multivariate analogue to the LB portmanteau test statistic for autocorrelation. The test statistic is given as follows:

$$\text{H}(m) = T^2 \sum_{t=1}^{M} (T-j)^{-1} tr\left\{C^{-1}(0)C(j)C^{-1}(0)C'(j)\right\}, \tag{3.2}$$

Table 3.3. Multivariate Ljung-Box Statistics for Returns and Squared Returns

Returns		Squared Returns		Critical Values
H(6)	239.62	**$H^2(6)$**	1522.70	72.15[54]
H(12)	335.00	**$H^2(12)$**	2339.24	133.26[108]
H(18)	406.32	**$H^2(18)$**	3058.04	192.70[162]
H(24)	457.54	**$H^2(24)$**	3650.41	251.29[216]

Note: H and H^2 equal the Hosking (1980) multivariate analogue to the LB-Q and LB-Q^2 tests for autocorrelation. Number of lags appears in parentheses. The 5-percent critical values appear with degrees of freedom in brackets.

where $C(j)$ equals the sample autocovariance matrix of order j. Under the null hypothesis of no dependence in the returns or squared returns, the test statistic is asymptotically distributed as a chi-square with n^2m degrees of freedom, where n equals the number of series and m equals the number of lags. Table 3.3 reports the observed $H(m)$ and $H^2(m)$ statistics calculated at six, twelve, eighteen, and twenty-four lags for the returns and squared returns. All test statistics prove statistically significant at the 1-percent level, implying that serial correlation in the returns and a significant amount of serial dependence in the squared returns exists. In sum, we find strong evidence of conditional heteroskedasticity.

The (unconditional) correlation coefficient of returns provides one indicator of the co-movements of international stock indices and a rough measure of market interdependence. The correlation coefficients between returns fall in the moderate range, but prove significant at the 1-percent level. The correlation between Mexico and US equals 0.529, slightly higher than the correlation between Mexico and Canada (0.474). The highest correlation, as expected, occurs between Canada and the US (0.691).

Chapter 4

COINTEGRATION ANALYSES

This Chapter implements our investigation of cointegration. That is, do the three NAFTA stock markets exhibit a long-run trend relationship between the stock market returns. Our analysis begins with tests for cointegration over the entire sample period. Next, we examine recursive cointegration tests. We estimate and test for cointegration over an initial sample period of daily data in 1992 and then extend the sample period one day at a time and re-estimate and retest for cointegration. Third, we consider rolling cointegration tests. We estimate and test for cointegration over an initial sample period of daily data from 1992 to 2002 and then move the sample forward by one day and eliminate the first day in the sample, keeping the sample size constant, and re-estimate and retest for cointegration. Rolling regressions keeps the power of the tests the same, whereas the recursive cointegration tests experiences a rise in the power of the test as the sample size grows. Fourth, we redo the estimation and cointegration tests for the whole sample period with the inclusion of endogenous structural breaks in the relationship. Finally, we evaluate threshold cointegration models.

4.1. THE JOHANSEN MULTIVARIATE APPROACH

If a long-run relationship exists between two or more variables, then bounds encompass any deviation from the long-run equilibrium path. If true, then the variables are cointegrated. We analyze the long-term relationship between the three North American stock markets, using the multivariate cointegration techniques of Johansen (1988, 1991) and Johansen and Juselius (1990). Their approach uses maximum likelihood (ML) estimators of the cointegrating vectors for a vector autoregressive process with Gaussian errors. This procedure incorporates the whole error structure of the underlying multivariate process, including different short-run and long-run dynamics of a system of economic variables. Cointegration allows an analysis of the equilibrium relationships among non-stationary series, while abstracting from the short-term deviations from that long-run equilibrium. This section briefly describes the estimation method and the empirical results.

Johansen and Juselius (1990) consider a p-dimensional, k^{th}-order unrestricted vector autoregression (VAR) as follows:

$$X_t = A_0 + A_1 X_{t-1} + \ldots + A_k X_{t-k} + \varepsilon_t \ t = 1,\ldots,T, \tag{4.1}$$

where X_t equals a $(p \ x \ 1)$ vector of non-stationary variables, A_i, $i = 1,\ldots,k$ equals a $(p \ x \ p)$ matrix of parameters, and ε_t equals a vector of innovations drawn from a p-dimensional i.i.d. normal distribution with mean zero and covariance Σ.

Letting Δ represent the first-difference operator, we can reformulate equation (4.1) as a VEC model as follows:

$$\Delta X_t = \Gamma_1 \Delta X_{t-1} + \ldots + \Gamma_{k-1} \Delta X_{t-k+1} + \Pi X_{t-1} + \varepsilon_t, \tag{4.2}$$

where $\Gamma_m = -I + \sum_{i=1}^{m} A_i$ for $m = 1,\ldots,k\text{-}1$, $\Pi = -I + \sum_{i=1}^{k} A_i$, and I equals the identity matrix.

We seek cointegration by examining the rank of Π since, as Johansen (1990, 1991) and Johansen and Juselius (1990) show, the rank r of Π determines the number of stationary linear combinations of X_t. Three possibilities exist. First, if the rank r of Π equals zero, the VEC model reduces to a standard vector autoregressive (VAR) model in first-differences. All elements of X_t are non-stationary [i.e., I(1)] and no stationary long-run relationships exist among them. Second, if Π possesses full rank, $r = p$, then all elements of X_t are stationary [i.e., I(0)] and no stochastic trends exist in the series, contrary to the original I(1) specification. Finally, if Π possesses rank $0 < r < p$, then r cointegrating vectors exist. The $(p \ x \ r)$ matrices α and β each of rank r exist such that $\Pi = \alpha\beta'$, where the columns of the matrix α equal adjustment factors and the rows of the matrix β equal the cointegrating vectors, where $\beta' X_t$ follows an I(0) (stationary) process even though each element of X_t includes individually I(1) (non-stationary) variables. The cointegrating vectors capture the long-run relationships in the system. Johansen (1988, 1991) shows that only the cointegration vectors in β enter equation (4.2), otherwise ΠX_{t-1} is not I(0). This implies effectively that the last (p - r) columns of α equal zero. Thus, the problem of determining how many $r \leq p$ cointegration vectors exist in β equivalently tests how many columns of α equal zero.

Johansen (1988, 1991) shows that the estimation procedure simplifies by reformulating model (4) as follows:

$$R_{0t} = \alpha\beta' R_{1t} + \zeta_t, \tag{4.3}$$

where R_{0t} and R_{1t} equal vectors of residuals from the auxiliary regressions:

$$\Delta X_t = \hat{\pi}_0 + \hat{\vartheta}_1 \Delta X_{t-1} + \hat{\vartheta}_2 \Delta X_{t-2} + \ldots + \hat{\vartheta}_{p-1} \Delta X_{t-(p-1)} + R_{0t}, \text{ and} \tag{4.4}$$

$$X_{t-1} = \hat{\theta}_0 + \hat{\xi}_1 \Delta X_{t-1} + \hat{\xi}_2 \Delta X_{t-2} + \ldots + \hat{\xi}_{p-1} \Delta X_{t-(p-1)} + R_{1t}. \tag{4.5}$$

We can estimate these two equations by ordinary least squares (OLS). The sample variance-covariance matrices of the OLS residuals R_{0t} and R_{1t} equal the following: $S_{11} = (1/T)\sum_{t=1}^{T} R_{1t} R'_{1t}$, $S_{00} = (1/T)\sum_{t=1}^{T} R_{0t} R'_{0t}$, $S_{01} = (1/T)\sum_{t=1}^{T} R_{0t} R'_{1t}$, $S_{10} = S'_{01}$.

The ML estimator of β in equation (4.1) comes from solving for the eigenvalues of the equation:

$$\left| \lambda S_{11} - S_{10} S_{00}^{-1} S_{01} \right| = 0, \tag{4.6}$$

which gives the p eigenvalues, $1 > \hat{\lambda}_1 > ... > \hat{\lambda}_p > 0$, and the corresponding eigenvectors $\hat{V} = (\hat{v}_1, ..., \hat{v}_p)$ normalized such that $\hat{V}'S_{11}\hat{V} = I$. The eigenvalues $\hat{\lambda}_1, ..., \hat{\lambda}_p$ correspond to the squared canonical correlations between the "levels" residuals and the "difference" residuals, as defined above. The eigenvectors $\hat{v}_1, ..., \hat{v}_p$ determine the linear combinations $\hat{v}_i' z_t$, $i = 1, ..., k$-1.

Johansen (1988, 1991) proposes two methods for testing for the number of cointegration vectors: the trace and maximum eigenvalue tests. The trace test equals a likelihood ratio test for maximum r cointegration vectors against the alternative of n vectors as follows:

$$\lambda_{\text{trace}} = -T \sum_{i=r+1}^{p} \ln(1 - \hat{\lambda}_i), \tag{4.7}$$

where $\hat{\lambda}_{r+1}, ..., \hat{\lambda}_n$ equal the (n-r) smallest eigenvalues of the squared canonical correlations. The maximum eigenvalue test possesses an identical null hypothesis, while the alternative hypothesis equals (r+1) cointegration vectors. That is,

$$\lambda_{\max} = -T \ln(1 - \hat{\lambda}_{r+1}), \tag{4.8}$$

where $\hat{\lambda}_{r+1}$ equals the largest eigenvalue. Both tests possess a non-standard asymptotic distribution. The critical values for λ_{trace} and $\lambda_{\max}$ come from MacKinnon et al. (1999), who compute numerical distribution functions of these two statistics. They find that the resultant critical values prove more reliable than those in Osterwald-Lenum (1992).

4.2. Empirical Results[1]

Cointegration analysis requires nonstationary variables. Traditional statistical tests used for inference assume stationary ergodic processes. The usual distributional results and tests of significance prove invalid and potentially

[1] We generated our results, using CATS in RATS (2005), version 2.

misleading, when considering non-stationary series. Unit-root tests provide a simple method for testing whether a series is non-stationary and, therefore, a useful check of appropriateness and statistical reliability of the time-series models. Previous studies find that many macroeconomic and financial time series, including stock price series, contain unit roots dominated by stochastic trends (Lee and Jeon, 1995). A necessary, but not sufficient, condition for cointegration requires that each of the stock price indices must conform to the same order of integration, or I(1) (Granger, 1986).

In the time-series literature, many ways exist to test for the stationarity in time-series variables, including several unit-root tests. The three most frequently used tests include, among others, the Dickey-Fuller (DF) test, the augmented Dickey-Fuller (ADF) test, and the Phillips-Perron (PP) test. The following discussion outlines the basic features of these unit-root tests. Consider a simple autoregressive process of order one, an AR(1), process:

$$y_t = \rho y_{t-1} + x_t'\gamma + \varepsilon_t, \qquad (4.9)$$

where x_t equals a vector of exogenous regressors, ρ and γ equal parameters that we estimate, and ε_t equals a stationary error term. If $|\rho| \geq 1$, then y_t is a nonstationary series with the variance of y_t increasing with time and approaching infinity. If, instead, $|\rho| < 1$, then y_t is a (trend-) stationary series. Thus, we can test the hypothesis of (trend-) stationarity by considering whether the absolute value of ρ strictly falls below one.

We perform the standard DF test by estimating equation (4.9) after subtracting y_{t-1} from both sides: That is,

$$y_t - y_{t-1} = \Delta y_t = \alpha y_{t-1} + x_t'\gamma + \varepsilon_t, \qquad (4.10)$$

where $\alpha = \rho - 1$.

Dickey and Fuller (DF, 1979) considered the following three different equations to test for the presence of unit roots:

$$\Delta y_t = \alpha y_{t-1} + \varepsilon_t; \qquad (4.11)$$

$$\Delta y_t = a_0 + \alpha y_{t-1} + \varepsilon_t \text{; and} \tag{4.12}$$

$$\Delta y_t = a_0 + a_1 t + \alpha y_{t-1} + \varepsilon_t . \tag{4.13}$$

The differences among these regression equations depend on the presence of a_0, a constant (drift), and $a_1 t$, a deterministic term (linear time trend).

The DF unit-root test considers the null hypothesis that $\alpha = 0$ versus the alternative that $\alpha < 0$. The test uses the conventional *t*-ratio for α, defined as $t_\alpha = \hat{\alpha} / se(\hat{\alpha})$ where $\hat{\alpha}$ equals the OLS estimate of α and $se(\hat{\alpha})$ equals the standard error of $\hat{\alpha}$. Dickey and Fuller (1979) show that under the null hypothesis of a unit root, t_α does not follow the conventional *t*-distribution and derive asymptotic values for each version of the test and various sample sizes.

Dickey and Fuller (1979) extend this test to higher-order autoregressive processes. This extended test, the augmented Dickey-Fuller (ADF) test, considers a pth-order autoregressive process, which modifies equations (13), (14), and (15) as follows:

$$\Delta y_t = \alpha y_{t-1} + \sum_{j=1}^{p} \gamma_j \Delta y_{t-j} + \varepsilon_t ; \tag{4.14}$$

$$\Delta y_t = a_0 + \alpha y_{t-1} + \sum_{j=1}^{p} \gamma_j \Delta y_{t-j} + \varepsilon_t \text{; and} \tag{4.15}$$

$$\Delta y_t = a_0 + a_1 t + \alpha y_{t-1} + \sum_{j=1}^{p} \gamma_j \Delta y_{t-j} + \varepsilon_t , \tag{4.16}$$

where a_0 and t equal a constant and a time trend, respectively. The asymptotic distribution of the ADF test does not depend on the number of lagged first differences included in the regression and maintains its validity in the presence of a moving average (MA) component (Said and Dickey, 1984).

One drawback exists, however, with both the DF and the ADF tests. To wit, the test statistics assume that the errors are statistically independent with constant variance. Phillips and Perron (PP, 1988) develop a test for unit roots that allows the errors to exhibit weak dependence and heterogeneity. The PP test uses the non-augmented DF test in equations (13), (14), and (15), but modifies the t-ratio for α so that serial correlation does not affect the asymptotic distribution of the test statistic. We write the PP test as follows:

$$\bar{t}_{\alpha} = t_{\alpha}\left(\frac{\gamma_0}{f_0}\right)^{1/2} - \frac{T(f_0 - \gamma_0)se(\hat{\alpha})}{2f_0^{1/2}s}, \quad (4.17)$$

where $\hat{\alpha}$ equals the estimate, t_{α} equals the t-ratio of $\hat{\alpha}$, $se(\hat{\alpha})$ equals the standard error of $\hat{\alpha}$, and s equals the standard error of the regression. The remaining terms, γ_0 and f_0, equal, respectively, a consistent estimate of the residual variance and an estimate of the residual spectrum at frequency zero. We calculate the residual variance as $(T-k)s^2/T$.

We use the ADF test (Dickey and Fuller, 1979), including a constant and a linear deterministic trend in the test equation. The lag length choice uses the Akaike information criterion (AIC). We also examine for unit roots in the series of the indices and the respective returns using the PP test (Phillips and Perron, 1988), which depends on a weaker assumption that the error terms do not necessarily conform to independently, identically distributed values. Monte Carlo studies suggest that the PP test possesses more power than the ADF test. The PP test also includes a constant and a linear deterministic trend in the test equation and employs the Bartlett kernel spectral estimation method with the Newey-West bandwidth.

Table 4.1 reports results of the unit-root analysis. The ADF tests suggest that each stock price index exhibits non-stationarity in levels and stationarity in first differences, indicating that all the stock price indices are I(1) series. The PP test results provide consistent findings with those of the ADF test. Further, the results of the ADF and PP tests prove robust to the exclusion of the linear deterministic trend. In sum, the findings of the ADF and PP tests consistently indicate I(1) stock index values (in natural logs) as well as I(0) stock return series, proving consistent with prior work. Since all the stock price indices are integrated of order one [i.e., I(1)], we can apply cointegration tests to determine whether long-run equilibrium relationships exist.

Table 4.1. Unit Root Tests

	Indices		Returns	
	ADF	**PP**	**ADF**	**PP**
S&P 500	-1.41	-1.23	-11.58	-63.84
S&P TSX	-2.18	-2.06	-10.68	-56.40
IPC	-2.54	-2.40	-11.48	-55.81

Note: ADF and PP equal the augmented Dickey-Fuller (1979) with a constant and a linear deterministic time trend and the Phillips-Perron (1988) tests for non-stationarity. The critical values for the ADF and PP tests equal -3.12, -3.41, and -3.96 at the 10-, 5-, and 1-percent levels, respectively.

The empirical implementation of the Johansen cointegration tests requires the determination of the appropriate lag length in the VAR model. The Monte-Carlo results in Cheung and Lai (1993) indicate that both the trace and maximal-eigenvalue statistics are robust to over-parameterization in k. For under-parameterization of k, however, a serious upward bias exists for both the trace and maximal-eigenvalue statistics, seriously distorting the cointegration tests. Thus, choosing less than the optimal value of k can affect our inferences concerning the cointegration rank and, hence, the number of potential cointegrating vectors in our model. The empirical results in Cheung and Lai (1993) also suggest that the lag selection criteria help to choose the right lag length.

We use the multivariate versions of the sequential modified likelihood ratio (LR) test statistic at the 5-percent level, the Akaike information criterion (AIC), the final prediction error (FPE), the Schwarz information criterion (SIC), and the Hannan-Quinn information criterion (HQ) to determine the lag length. These information criteria represent various prediction risk estimates proposed in the statistical literature (Lutkepohl, 1991) for model selection (in the linear case).

The sequential modified likelihood ratio (LR) tests the hypothesis that the coefficients on lag p jointly equal zero:

$$\mathrm{LR} = \left(T-k\right)\left\{\log\left|\hat{\Omega}_{p-1}\right| - \log\left|\hat{\Omega}_{p}\right|\right\} \tag{4.18}$$

which approximates a $\chi^2(k^2)$ distribution, where k equals the number of parameters under the alternative. The test compares the modified LR statistics to the 5-perecent critical values, starting from the maximum lag (chosen a priori) and decreasing the lag one at a time until a rejection is obtained.

Akaike (1974, 1978, 1979), Schwarz (1978), and Hannan and Quinn (1979) develop model selection criteria, using a Bayesian approach which incorporates a large penalty factor for over fitting the model. These criteria are defined as follows:

$$\mathrm{FPE} = \left[\left(1+\frac{k}{T}\right) \Big/ \left(1-\frac{k}{T}\right) \right] \left|\hat{\Omega}\right|, \tag{4.19}$$

$$\mathrm{AIC} = -2(L/T) + 2(k/T), \tag{4.20}$$

$$\mathrm{SIC} = -2(L/T) + k\log(T)/T \text{, and} \tag{4.21}$$

$$\mathrm{HQIC} = -2(L/T) + 2k\log\left[\log(T)\right]/T, \tag{4.22}$$

where L equals the value of the log of the likelihood function with k parameters, estimated using T observations, and $\left|\hat{\Omega}\right|$ equals the determinant of the variance-covariance matrix of the residuals.

Table 4.2 reports the results of our lag-length analysis. The first three criteria (i.e., LR, FPE, and AIC) suggest a model with 3 lags, while the last two criteria (i.e., SIC and HQIC) suggest a model with 1 lag. As an additional criterion, we also check for residual autocorrelation in all estimated models. Since the residuals from the model with 3 lags do not exhibit significant autocorrelations and because of the Monte Carlo findings of Cheung and Lai (1993), we proceed the analysis with a VAR specification of 3 lags.

Tables 4.3, 4.4, and 4.5 report the results of the Johansen trivariate cointegration tests, where we consider three alternative models that differ on the trend assumptions. In Model 1, the series exclude deterministic trends and the cointegrating equations include intercepts. In Model 2, the series include deterministic trends, but the cointegrating equations include only intercepts. In Model 3, both the series and the cointegrating equations include linear deterministic trends.

Table 4.2. VAR Lag Order Selection Criteria

Lag	LogL	LR	FPE	AIC	SIC	HQIC
0	-15953.4	NA	0.929	8.4403	8.4452	8.4421
1	-15867.7	171.32	0.8923	8.3997	**8.4195**	**8.4067**
2	-15852.9	29.44	0.8896	8.3967	8.4313	8.4090
3	-15842.5	**20.88**	**0.8889**	**8.3959**	8.4454	8.4135
4	-15835.6	13.60	0.8900	8.3970	8.4614	8.4199
5	-15830.6	9.963	0.8918	8.3991	8.4784	8.4273
6	-15826.5	8.22	0.8941	8.4017	8.4958	8.4352
7	-15818.6	15.73	0.8947	8.4023	8.5112	8.4410
8	-15812.5	12.17	0.8960	8.4038	8.5276	8.4478

Note: LogL, LR, FPE, AIC, SIC, and HQIC equal the log likelihood value, the likelihood ratio, the final prediction error, the Akaike information criterion, the Schwartz information criterion, and the Hannan-Quinn information criterion.

Table 4.3. Johansen Tests of Cointegration – Model 1

		Trace Statistic for Cointegrating Rank		
H_0:	**H_A:**	**Eigenvalue**	**Trace Statistic**	**5% Critical Value**
$r = 0$	$r \geq 1$	0.0039	24.5335	34.9100
$r \leq 1$	$r \geq 2$	0.0018	9.7345	19.9600
$r \leq 2$	$r = 3$	0.0008	2.9302	9.2400
		Maximum Eigenvalue Statistic for Cointegrating Rank		
H_0:	**H_A:**	**Eigenvalue**	**Maximum Eigenvalue**	**5% Critical Value**
$r = 0$	$r = 1$	0.0039	14.7990	22.0000
$r \leq 1$	$r = 2$	0.0018	6.8043	15.6700
$r \leq 2$	$r = 3$	0.0008	2.9302	9.2400

Note: H_0 and H_A equal the null and alternative hypotheses. In Model 1, the series exclude deterministic trends and the cointegrating equations include intercepts.

Table 4.4. Johansen Tests of Cointegration – Model 2

		Trace Statistic for Cointegrating Rank		
H_0:	H_A:	Eigenvalue	Trace Statistic	5% Critical Value
$r=0$	$r\geq 1$	0.0035	16.6024	29.7900
$r\leq 1$	$r\geq 2$	0.0008	3.1710	15.4900
$r\leq 2$	$r=3$	0.0000	0.0077	3.8400
		Maximum Eigenvalue Statistic for Cointegrating Rank		
H_0:	H_A:	**Eigenvalue**	**Maximum Eigenvalue**	**5% Critical Value**
$r=0$	$r=1$	0.0035	13.4314	21.1316
$r\leq 1$	$r=2$	0.0008	3.1633	14.2646
$r\leq 2$	$r=3$	0.0000	0.0077	3.8415

Note: See Table 4.3. In Model 2, the series include deterministic trends, but the cointegrating equations only include intercepts.

Table 4.5. Johansen Tests of Cointegration – Model 3

		Trace Statistic for Cointegrating Rank		
H_0:	H_A:	Eigenvalue	Trace Statistic	5% Critical Value
$r=0$	$r\geq 1$	0.0050	27.2579	42.9152
$r\leq 1$	$r\geq 2$	0.0014	8.3383	25.8721
$r\leq 2$	$r=3$	0.0008	3.1625	12.5179
		Maximum Eigenvalue Statistic for Cointegrating Rank		
H_0:	H_A:	**Eigenvalue**	**Maximum Eigenvalue**	**5% Critical Value**
$r=0$	$r=1$	0.0050	18.9196	25.8232
$r\leq 1$	$r=2$	0.0014	5.1759	19.3870
$r\leq 2$	$r=3$	0.0008	3.1625	12.5179

Note: See Table 4.3. In Model 3, the series and the cointegrating equations include deterministic trends.

Johansen (1992) argues that the presence or absence of deterministic components in the cointegration model can bias tests for cointegration and emphasizes the need to test the joint hypothesis of both the rank order and the deterministic components based on the Pantula principle. This procedure (principle) involves running a series of joint hypotheses about the number of cointegrating relationships as well as the presence of deterministic terms. We follow this method by running sequential tests from the most restrictive model (*rank* = 0, Model 1) to the least restrictive model (*rank* = 2, Model 3) and selecting a model for which we do not reject the null hypothesis in the first instance. The Pantula principle does elicit some controversy. Hjelm and Johansson (2005), for example, examine, using Monte-Carlo simulation, the properties of the Pantula principle for the simultaneous determination of rank and deterministic components and find that within the Johansen methodology, the Pantula principle heavily biases the outcome toward choosing the model with an unrestricted constant, when the true model contains a restricted trend. For this reason, we choose to present all three models.

In each table, r measures the rank of the Π matrix (i.e., the order of cointegration). MacKinnon et al. (1999) provide the critical values. The results of the cointegration tests prove robust to the different specifications of the deterministic components. The trace and maximum eigenvalue tests cannot reject the null hypothesis of no-cointegration among the stock indices of Canada, Mexico, and the US ($r = 0$) against the alternative hypothesis of one or more cointegrating vectors ($r > 0$) at the 5-percent level. That is, the stock indices of the three countries in North America do not share long-run equilibrium relationships. These results may conflict with those of Ortiz et al. (2008), Darrat and Zhang (2005), and Gilmore and McManus (2004). Our sample considers daily data over the whole sample period. Ortiz et al. (2008) also employ daily data. They find a long-run trend relationship between the three markets and we do not. Darrat and Zhang (2005) use weekly data. Finally, Gilmore and McManus (2004) examine weekly and monthly data. Thus, Darrat and Zhang (2005) and Gilmore and McManus (2004) find a long-run trend relationship in the NAFTA period may reflect differences in sample period and/or differences in data frequency.

We test for the normality of the residuals, using the Doornik-Hansen (1994) method and reject the null hypothesis of normality at the 1-percent level. Since non-normality of residuals does not bias the results for the Johansen's cointegration tests, the test results prove valid (Gonzalo, 1994). We also test for ARCH effects in the residuals, using Hosking's (1980) multivariate tests and reject the null hypothesis of no ARCH effects at the 1-percent level. Rahbek, Hansen, and Dennis (2002) and Juselius (2006), however, report that the cointegration tests prove robust against moderate ARCH.

Table 4.6. Johansen Tests of Cointegration: Mexico-Canada – Model 1

		Trace Statistic for Cointegrating Rank		
H_0:	**H_A:**	**Eigenvalue**	**Trace Statistic**	**5% Critical Value**
$r=0$	$r\geq1$	0.0026	15.1069	20.2618
$r\leq1$	$r\geq2$	0.0013	5.1293	9.1645
		Maximum Eigenvalue Statistic for Cointegrating Rank		
H_0:	**H_A:**	**Eigenvalue**	**Maximum Eigenvalue**	**5% Critical Value**
$r=0$	$r=1$	0.0026	9.9775	15.8921
$r\leq1$	$r=2$	0.0013	5.1293	9.1645

Note: H_0 and H_A equal the null and alternative hypotheses. In Model 1, the series exclude deterministic trends and the cointegrating equations include intercepts.

Table 4.7. Johansen Tests of Cointegration: Mexico-Canada – Model 2

		Trace Statistic for Cointegrating Rank		
H_0:	**H_A:**	**Eigenvalue**	**Trace Statistic**	**5% Critical Value**
$r=0$	$r\geq1$	0.0019	7.2870	15.4947
$r\leq1$	$r\geq2$	0.0000	0.0086	3.8414
		Maximum Eigenvalue Statistic for Cointegrating Rank		
H_0:	**H_A:**	**Eigenvalue**	**Maximum Eigenvalue**	**5% Critical Value**
$r=0$	$r=1$	0.0019	7.2784	14.2646
$r<1$	$r=2$	0.0000	0.0086	3.8414

Note: See Table 4.6. In Model 2, the series include deterministic trends, but the cointegrating equations only include intercepts.

We also test for pairwise cointegration. The bivariate results, presented in Tables 4.6, 4.7, and 4.8 for Mexico and Canada, Tables 4.9, 4.10, and 4.11 for Canada and the US, and Tables 4.12, 4.13, and 4.14 for the Mexico and the US, consistently fail to reject the hypothesis of no cointegration.

Table 4.8. Johansen Tests of Cointegration: Mexico-Canada – Model 3

		Trace Statistic for Cointegrating Rank		
H_0:	H_A:	Eigenvalue	Trace Statistic	5% Critical Value
$r=0$	$r \geq 1$	0.0024	14.2687	25.8721
$r \leq 1$	$r \geq 2$	0.0013	4.9820	12.5179
		Maximum Eigenvalue Statistic for Cointegrating Rank		
H_0:	**H_A:**	**Eigenvalue**	**Maximum Eigenvalue**	**5% Critical Value**
$r=0$	$r=1$	0.0024	9.2867	19.3870
$r \leq 1$	$r=2$	0.0013	4.9820	12.5179

Note: See Table 4.6. In Model 3, the series and the cointegrating equations include deterministic trends.

Table 4.9. Johansen Tests of Cointegration: Canada-US – Model 1

		Trace Statistic for Cointegrating Rank		
H_0:	H_A:	Eigenvalue	Trace Statistic	5% Critical Value
$r=0$	$r \geq 1$	0.0017	8.8022	20.2618
$r \leq 1$	$r \geq 2$	0.0005	2.2362	9.1645
		Maximum Eigenvalue Statistic for Cointegrating Rank		
H_0:	**H_A:**	**Eigenvalue**	**Maximum Eigenvalue**	**5% Critical Value**
$r=0$	$r=1$	0.0017	6.5660	15.8921
$r \leq 1$	$r=2$	0.0005	2.2362	9.1645

Note: See Table 4.6. In Model 1, the series exclude deterministic trends and the cointegrating equations include intercepts.

Table 4.10. Johansen Tests of Cointegration: Canada-US – Model 2

		Trace Statistic for Cointegrating Rank		
H_0:	H_A:	Eigenvalue	Trace Statistic	5% Critical Value
$r=0$	$r \geq 1$	0.0007	3.4458	15.4947
$r \leq 1$	$r \geq 2$	0.0001	0.6251	3.8414
		Maximum Eigenvalue Statistic for Cointegrating Rank		

H_0:	H_A:	Eigenvalue	Maximum Eigenvalue	5% Critical Value
$r=0$	$r=1$	0.0007	2.8207	14.2646
$r\leq1$	$r=2$	0.0001	0.6251	3.8414

Note: See Table 4.6. In Model 2, the series include deterministic trends, but the cointegrating equations only include intercepts.

Table 4.11. Johansen Tests of Cointegration: Canada-US – Model 3

		Trace Statistic for Cointegrating Rank		
H_0:	H_A:	Eigenvalue	Trace Statistic	5% Critical Value
$r=0$	$r\geq1$	0.0013	7.9325	25.8721
$r\leq1$	$r\geq2$	0.0007	2.7994	12.5179
		Maximum Eigenvalue Statistic for Cointegrating Rank		
H_0:	H_A:	Eigenvalue	Maximum Eigenvalue	5% Critical Value
$r=0$	$r=1$	0.0013	5.1331	19.3870
$r\leq1$	$r=2$	0.0007	2.7994	12.5179

Note: See Table 4.6. In Model 3, the series and the cointegrating equations include deterministic trends.

Table 4.12. Johansen Tests of Cointegration: US-Mexico – Model 1

		Trace Statistic for Cointegrating Rank		
H_0:	H_A:	Eigenvalue	Trace Statistic	5% Critical Value
$r=0$	$r\geq1$	0.0021	10.1263	20.2618
$r\leq1$	$r\geq2$	0.0005	2.2201	9.1645
		Maximum Eigenvalue Statistic for Cointegrating Rank		
H_0:	H_A:	Eigenvalue	Maximum Eigenvalue	5% Critical Value
$r=0$	$r=1$	0.0021	7.9062	15.8921
$r\leq1$	$r=2$	0.0005	2.2201	9.1645

Note: See Table 4.6. In Model 1, the series exclude deterministic trends and the cointegrating equations include intercepts.

Table 4.13. Johansen Tests of Cointegration: US-Mexico – Model 2

		Trace Statistic for Cointegrating Rank		
H_0:	**H_A:**	**Eigenvalue**	**Trace Statistic**	**5% Critical Value**
$r=0$	$r \geq 1$	0.0006	2.5447	15.4947
$r \leq 1$	$r \geq 2$	0.0000	0.0099	3.8414
		Maximum Eigenvalue Statistic for Cointegrating Rank		
H_0:	**H_A:**	**Eigenvalue**	**Maximum Eigenvalue**	**5% Critical Value**
$r=0$	$r=1$	0.0007	2.5348	14.2646
$r \leq 1$	$r=2$	0.0001	0.0099	3.8414

Note: See Table 4.6. In Model 2, the series include deterministic trends, but the cointegrating equations only include intercepts.

Table 4.14. Johansen Tests of Cointegration: US-Mexico – Model 3

		Trace Statistic for Cointegrating Rank		
H_0:	**H_A:**	**Eigenvalue**	**Trace Statistic**	**5% Critical Value**
$r=0$	$r \geq 1$	0.0018	9.3406	25.8721
$r \leq 1$	$r \geq 2$	0.0006	2.5009	12.5179
		Maximum Eigenvalue Statistic for Cointegrating Rank		
H_0:	**H_A:**	**Eigenvalue**	**Maximum Eigenvalue**	**5% Critical Value**
$r=0$	$r=1$	0.0018	6.8396	19.3870
$r \leq 1$	$r=2$	0.0006	2.5009	12.5179

Note: See Table 4.6. In Model 3, the series and the cointegrating equations include deterministic trends.

4.3. Recursive Cointegration Analysis

The stock markets of North America experienced frequent and substantial external and internal shocks during the 1992 to 2008 period. They include, among others, the Asian financial crisis of 1997, the Peso crisis of 1994, the Russian financial crisis of 1997, the stock market crash of 2000, and the September 11, 2001 attacks. This history suggests that finding empirical evidence to support one stable long-run relationship between the three markets may prove unlikely. Given the lack of support for a long-run relationship between the three North-American indices and the conflicting past evidence in the literature, the issue of temporal stability of the cointegration relationship warrants further examination. That is, we may find periods of time when a long-run relationship did exist.

Rangvid and Sorensen (2002) argue that conventional cointegration tests can only investigate whether the equity markets are integrated. If, however, we want to test econometrically whether the particular time series converge toward integration, then tests that do not permit the time disparity in the underlying data-generating process will bias the test toward rejecting cointegration. Thus, it appears desirable to use methods that explicitly incorporate the possibility of changes in the parameters of the underlying statistical model so that the process of convergence can occur. For this reason, we use time varying multivariate cointegration techniques in this section to analyze the dynamics of the process of integration of the three North-American markets. The time-varying formulation appears particularly suitable for our analysis, since the financial integration process may progress at different speeds and to different extents in each of the three equity markets.

In what follows, we perform dynamic cointegration analysis, using the recursive methods of Hansen and Johansen (1999). Hansen and Johansen (1999) analyze not only the extent, but also the dynamics, of the long-run relationships. They perform the analysis for an initial period and then update as new data augment the initial sample. Specifically, they compute tests statistics over the initial chosen sample 1, ..., T_1 where $T_1 < T$, extend the sample by one period and recalculate the statistics for the period 1 to (T_1+1), and so on until they exhaust the entire sample at T.

We estimate the recursive forward cointegration analysis under two VAR representations of equation (4.2). First, in the unrestricted or "X-representation," we re-estimate all the parameters of the VEC model during the sequence of recursive estimations. Second, in the restricted or "R-representation," we hold the short-term parameters Γ_i fixed to their full sample values and only re-estimate the long-run parameters in equation (4.2). In the "R-representation," rejections of stability reflect changes in the long-run structure, while in the "X-representation," rejections of stability reflect either shifts in the short-run dynamics or changes in the long-run structure. We employ three tests as follows: (1) the fluctuation test of the eigenvalues; (2) the test of β constancy, and 3) the trace test statistics.

Hansen and Johansen (1999) suggest a preliminary graphical procedure to assess the constancy of the long-run parameters over time in cointegrated vector autoregressive models. The procedure uses recursive estimates of the r largest eigenvalues, which provide information about the adjustment coefficients α_i and the cointegrating vectors β_i. The non-constancy of these parameters will, thus, reflect the time path of the estimated eigenvalues. We transform the eigenvalues λ_i $i = 1, \ldots, r$ into $\xi_i = \ln(\lambda_i / 1 - \lambda_i)$ to obtain a better approximation of their limiting distribution.

Figure 4.1 presents the results for the three estimated cointegration models and, although not a formal test of parameter stability, they indicate non-constancy of the parameters. We use

the one-year period in 1992 as the base period. In all three models, the estimates of ξ_1 decrease and stabilize in the second half of the sample. In the first half of the sample, however, large changes in ξ_1 occur, suggesting that some observations, especially in 1995 and 2000 exert a larger effect on parameter estimates.

Transformed Eigenvalues: Model 1

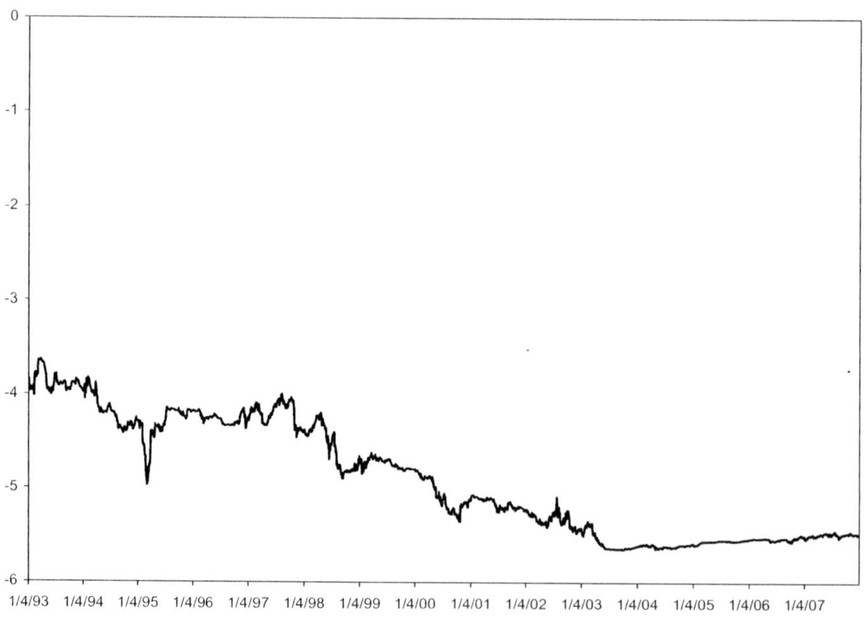

Transformed Eigenvalues: Model 2

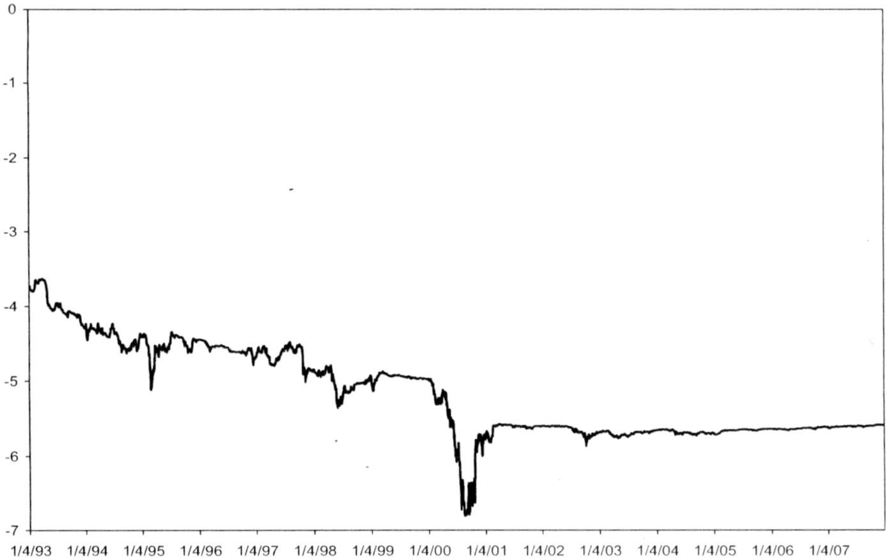

Transformed Eigenvalues: Model 3

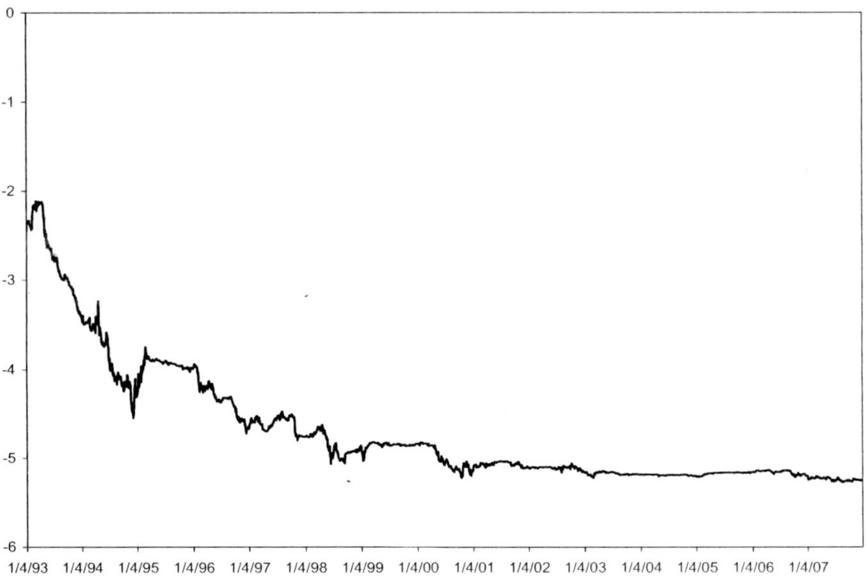

Figure 4.1. Time Path of the Transformed Eigenvalue $\xi_t = ln(\lambda_t / 1 - \lambda_t)$.

Following Hansen and Johansen (1999), we use the time path of the transformed estimated eigenvalues to construct the fluctuation test of the eigenvalues. The eigenvalues constancy test plots the sample path of the $\tau_i(t_1)$ defined as follows:

$$\tau_i(t_1) = \frac{t}{T}\left|\left(T^{-1}\Sigma_{ii}^{0}\right)^{-\frac{1}{2}}\xi_i\right|, \; i = 1,\ldots,r \text{ and } t_1 = 1, \ldots, T_1, \tag{4.23}$$

where Σ_{ii}^{0} equals the variance of the transformed eigenvalues. This supremum test provides a rather conservative signal, implying that rejecting the test provides a strong signal of non-constant eigenvalues (Juselius, 2006).

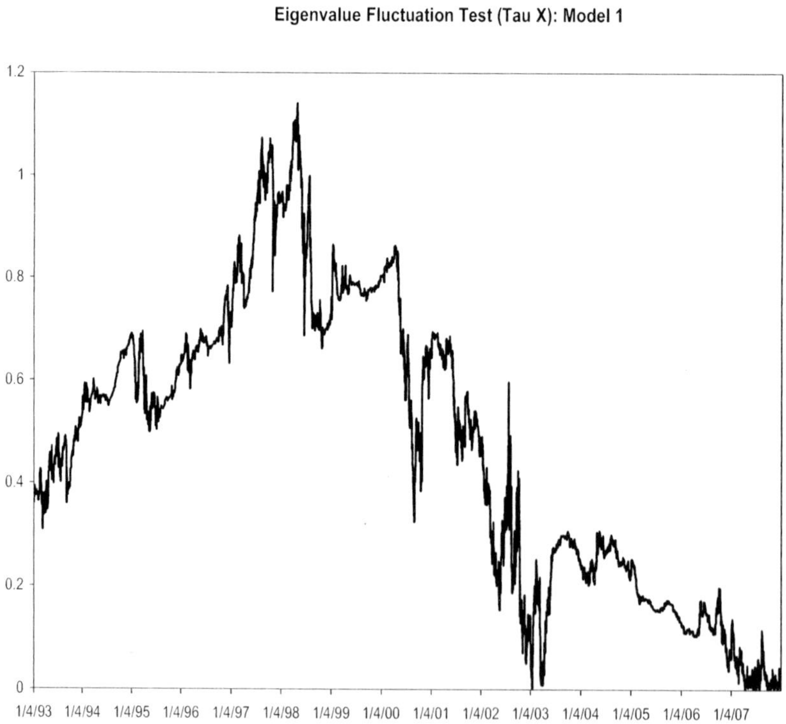

Figure 4.2. Fluctuation Tests of the Transformed First Eigenvalue – Model 1.

Figures 4.2, 4.3, and 4.4 present both the X- and R-representations of the test results for each of the estimated models. We calculate the test for the first eigenvalue. For ease of interpretation, we rescale the calculated statistics by the 5-percent critical value (1.36) of their asymptotic distribution (Ploberger et al., 1989). Rescaled values greater than 1 at a given data point provide evidence against the hypothesis of a constant eigenvalue at that data point. We reject the hypothesis of constant eigenvalues, because of the fluctuation either in the 1997-1998 Asian-financial-crisis period for Model 1, the 2000-2001 stock-market-crash period for Model 2, or the 1995-1996 Peso-crisis period for Model 3.

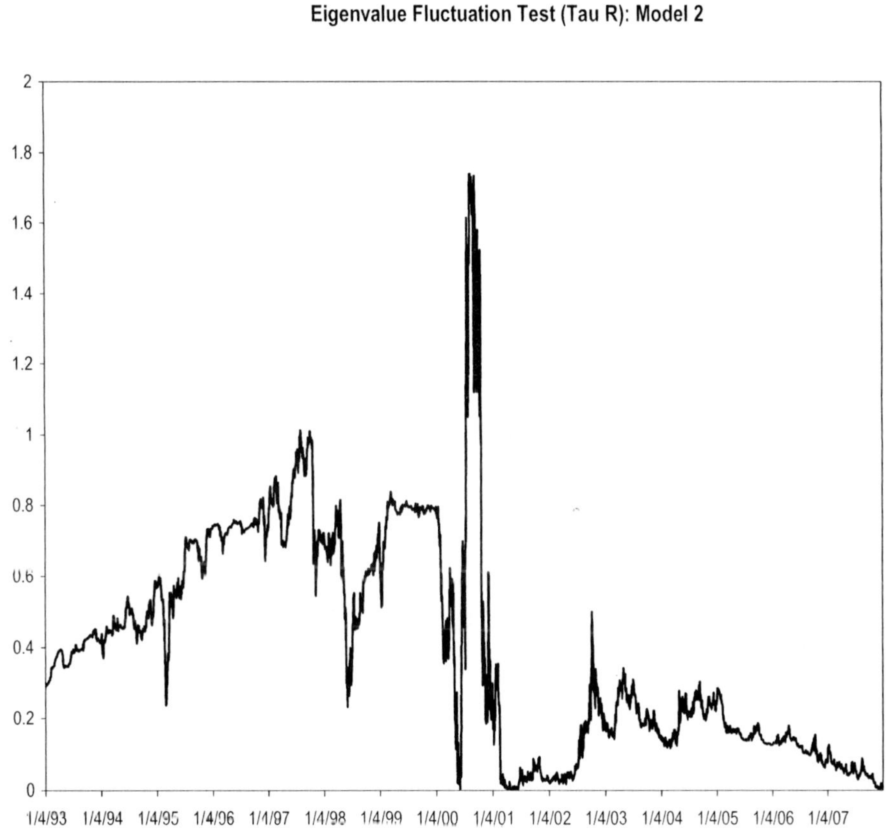

Figure 4.3. (Continued)

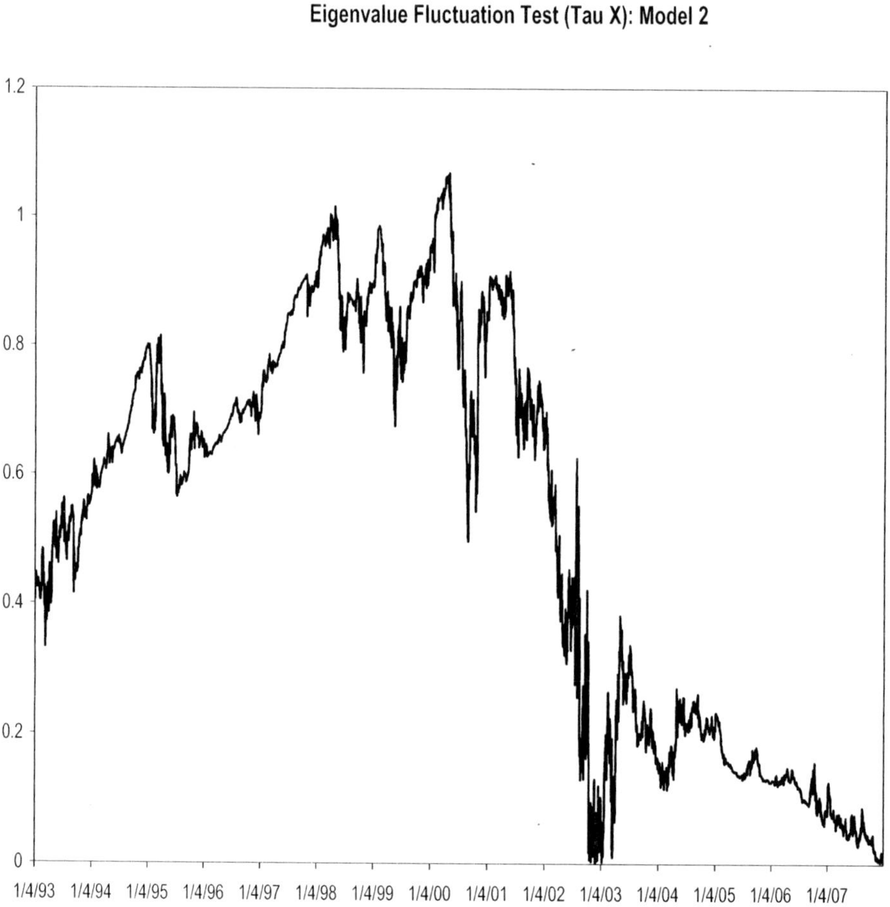

Figure 4.3. Fluctuation Tests of the Transformed Largest Eigenvalue – Model 2.

We next examine the constancy of β (Hansen and Johansen, 1999; Juselius, 2006), by recursively testing if the full-sample estimate of β, denoted by β_0, falls in the space spanned by $\hat{\beta}^{(t_1)}$, where $\hat{\beta}^{(t_1)}$ equals the estimate of β based on the period chosen for comparison. The test requires that the rank of Π equals $p_1 < r$. The test statistic equals the following:

$$-2\log Q(H_\beta|\beta^{(t_1)}) = t_1 \sum_{i=1}^{r} \ln \frac{1-\hat{\rho}_i^{(t_1)}}{1-\hat{\lambda}_i^{(t_1)}}, \tag{4.24}$$

where $\hat{\lambda}_i^{(t_1)}$ solves the eigenvalue problem $\left|\lambda S_{11}^{(t_1)} - S_{10}^{(t_1)}(S_{00}^{(t_1)})^{-1} S_{01}^{(t_1)}\right| = 0$ and $\hat{\rho}_i^{(t_1)}$ solves the eigenvalue problem $\left|\rho\beta_0' S_{11}^{(t_1)}\beta_0 - \beta_0' S_{10}^{(t_1)}(S_{00}^{(t_1)})^{-1} S_{01}^{(t_1)}\beta_0\right| = 0$ for the various samples considered. The statistic is asymptotically distributed as χ^2 with $r(p_1 - r)$ degrees of freedom, where p_1 equals the dimension of β and r equals the rank of the cointegration matrix.

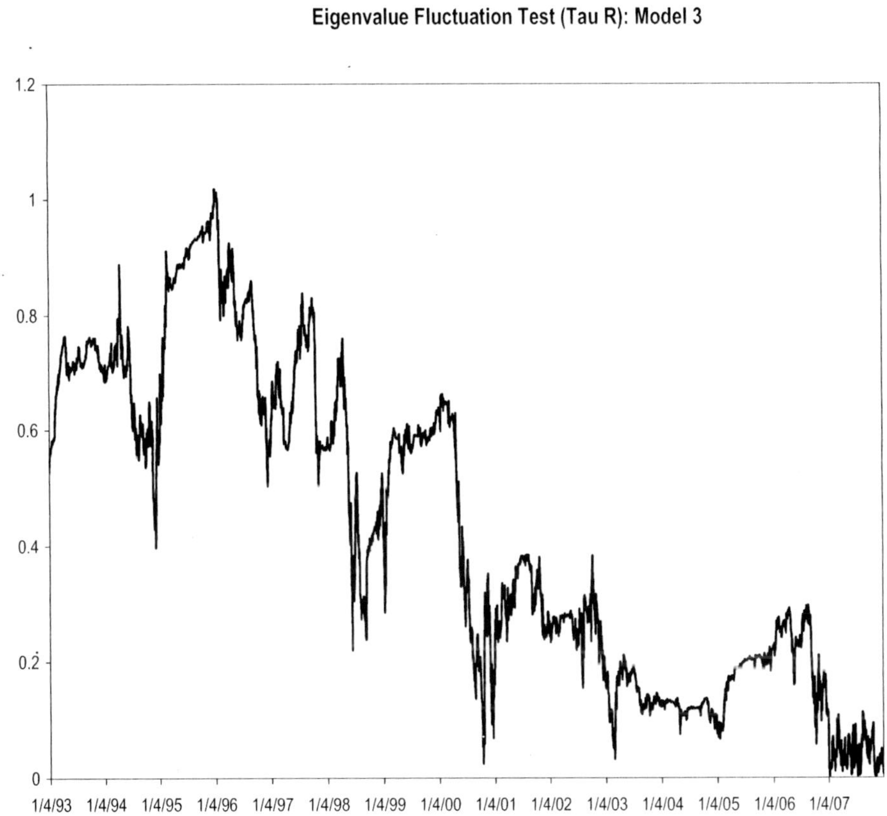

Figure 4.4. (Continued)

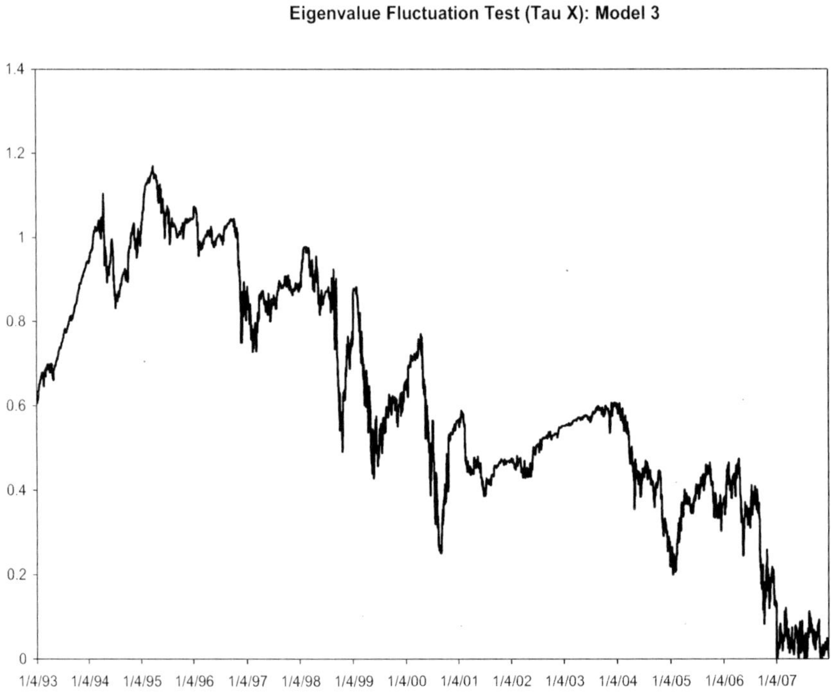

Figure 4.4. Fluctuation Tests of the Transformed Largest Eigenvalue – Model 3.

Figures 4.5, 4.6, and 4.7 illustrate the time path of the tests for $\beta_0 \in \text{span}\left\{\hat{\beta}^{(n)}\right\}$ for each of the three models, scaled by the 5-percent critical value. Test values below one indicate non-rejection of the null hypothesis that the β estimates for the corresponding recursive estimation period do not statistically differ from the β estimates derived from the full sample at the 5-percent significance level. Each figure portrays both the X- and R-representations. For both representations, the test statistics fluctuate throughout most of the estimation period, although exceeding 1 in only a few instances. In Model 1, for example, instability occurs mainly in the 1995-to-2000 Asian-financial-crisis period. Conversely, Model 2 rejects constant β estimates in the 1993-to-1995 Peso-crisis period and in the 2000-to-2001 stock-market-crash period. Finally, Model 3 detects instability mainly in the 1993-to-1996 Peso-crisis period. Thus, as we add observations from these sub-periods to the base sample, the estimated β parameters prove time varying.

Eigenvalue Fluctuation Test (Tau R): Model 1

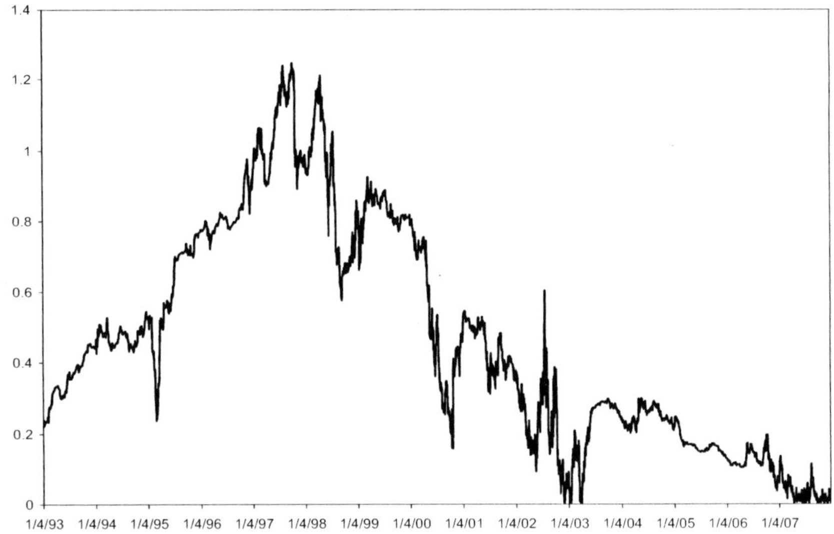

Test of Beta(t) = 'Known Beta'(R): Model 1

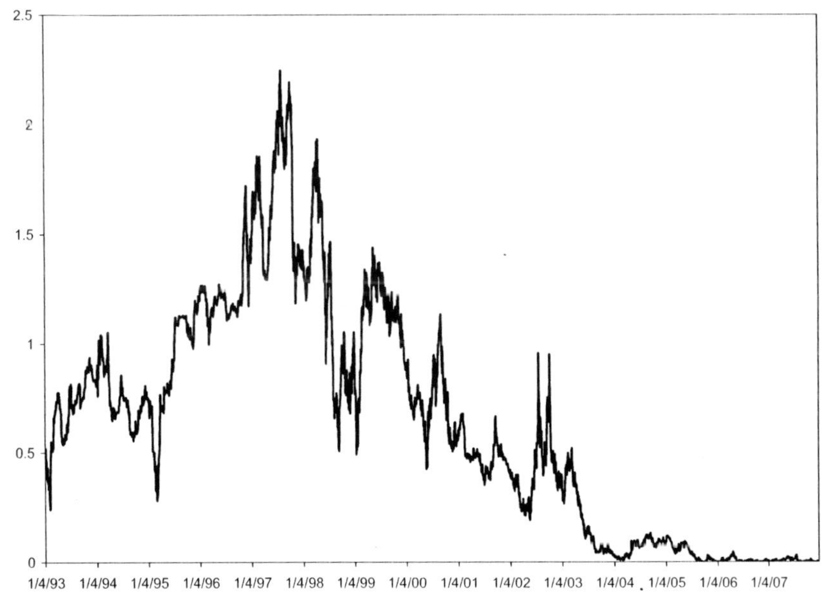

Figure 4.5. (Continued)

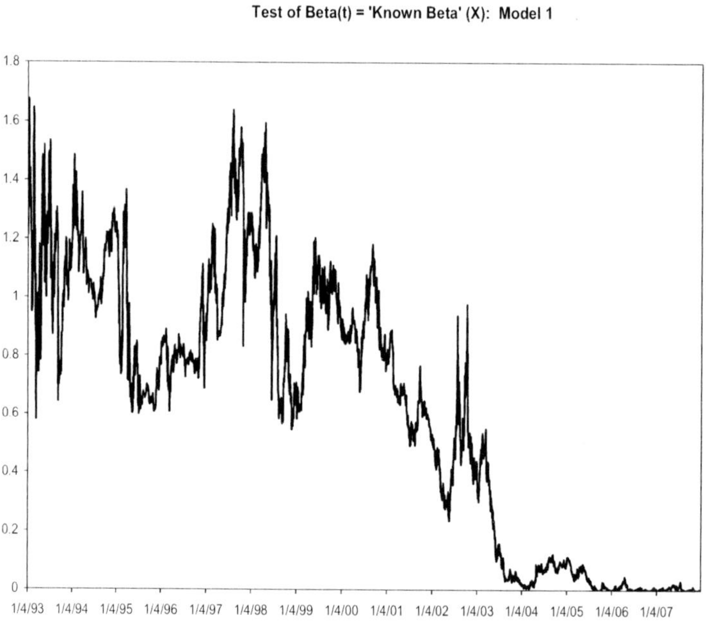

Figure 4.5. Time Path of the Tests for $\boldsymbol{\beta}_0 \in \text{Span}\left\{\hat{\boldsymbol{\beta}}^{(t_i)}\right\}$ – Model 1.

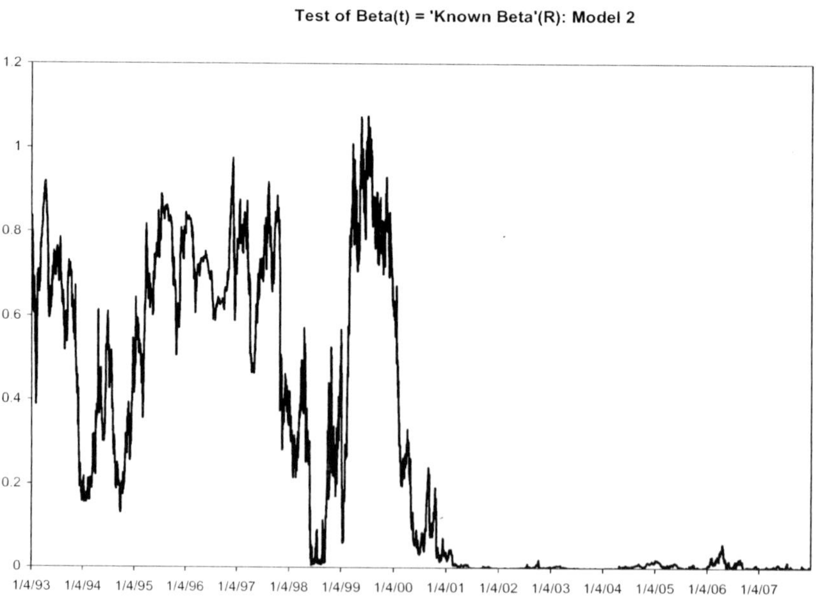

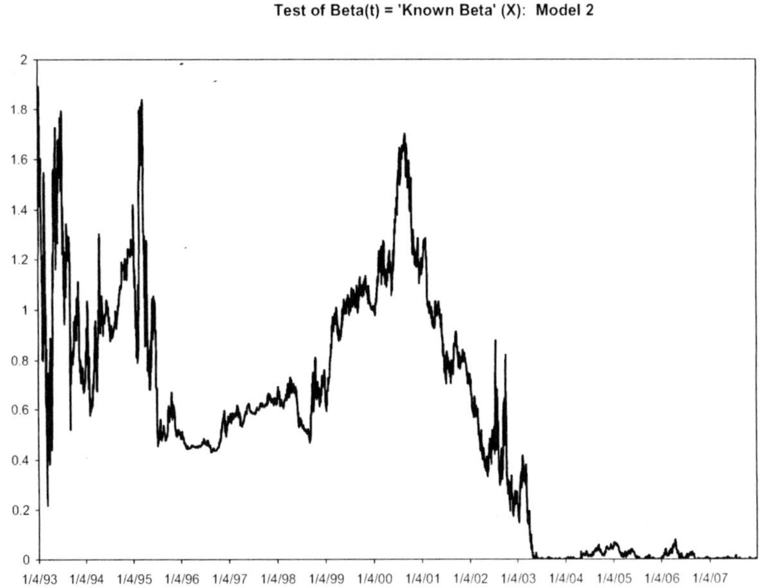

Figure 4.6. Time Path of the Tests for $\boldsymbol{\beta}_0 \in \text{Span}\left\{\hat{\boldsymbol{\beta}}^{(t_i)}\right\}$ – Model 2.

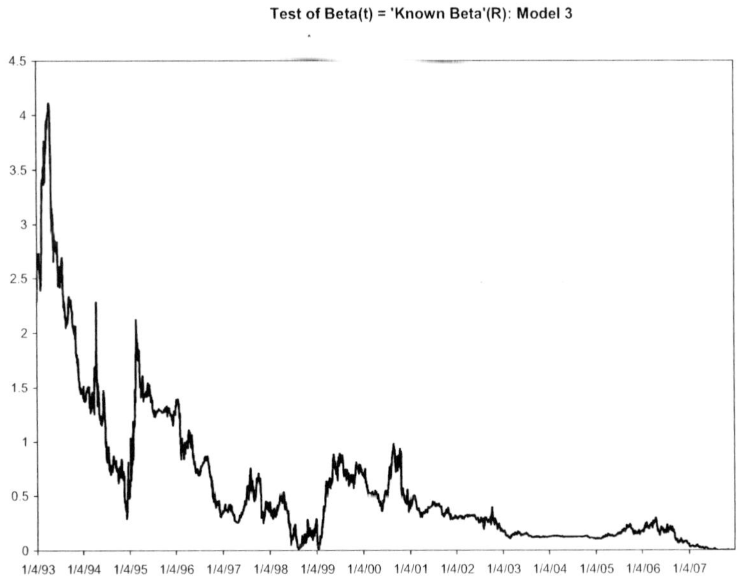

Figure 4.7. (Continued)

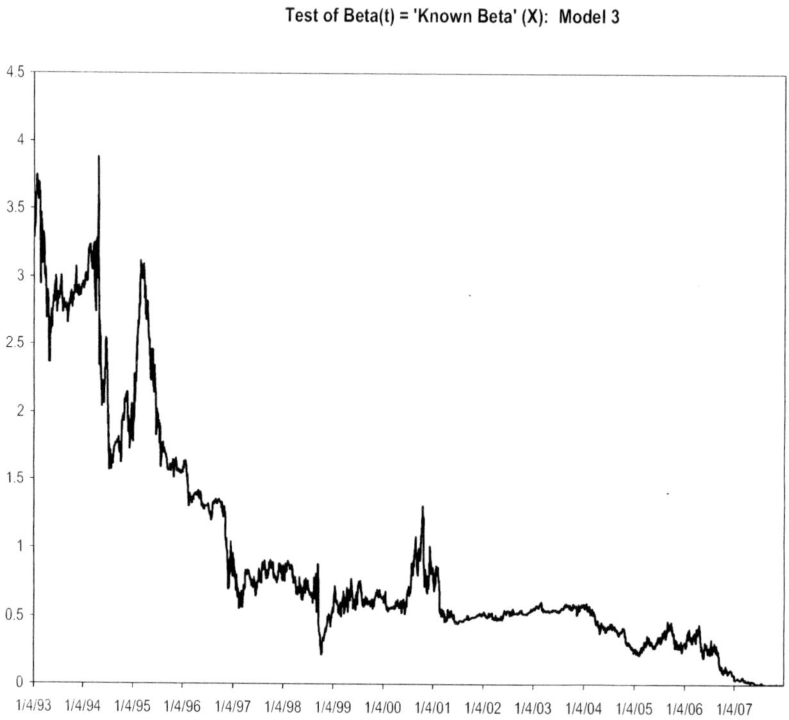

Figure 4.7. Time Path of the Tests for $\boldsymbol{\beta}_0 \in \text{Span}\left\{\hat{\boldsymbol{\beta}}^{(t_1)}\right\}$ – Model 3.

We finally consider a recursive trace test as follows:

$$\tau(r) = -t_1 \sum_{i=1}^{r} \ln(1-\hat{\lambda}_i) \quad r = 1,\ldots,p, \; t_1 = T_1,\ldots,T. \tag{4.25}$$

For each of the three models, Figures 4.8, 4.9, and 4.10 illustrate the time path of the recursive trace test scaled by the 5-percent critical value. Each figure presents two sets of recursive trace tests. The first set includes three graphs. These graphs show the path of the trace tests for, respectively, zero, one, and two cointegrating vectors in the unrestricted or "X-representation;" The second set comprises the last three graphs, which show the path of the tests for, respectively, zero, one, and two cointegrating vectors in the restricted or "R-representation."

Trace Test Statistic (X, p - r = 3): Model 1

Trace Test Statistic (X, p - r = 2): Model 1

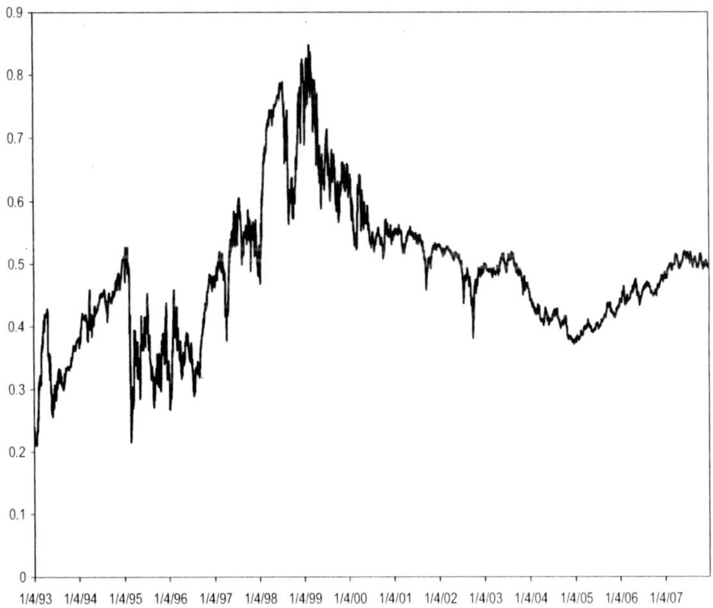

Figure 4.8. (Continued)

Trace Test Statistic (X, p - r = 1): Model 1

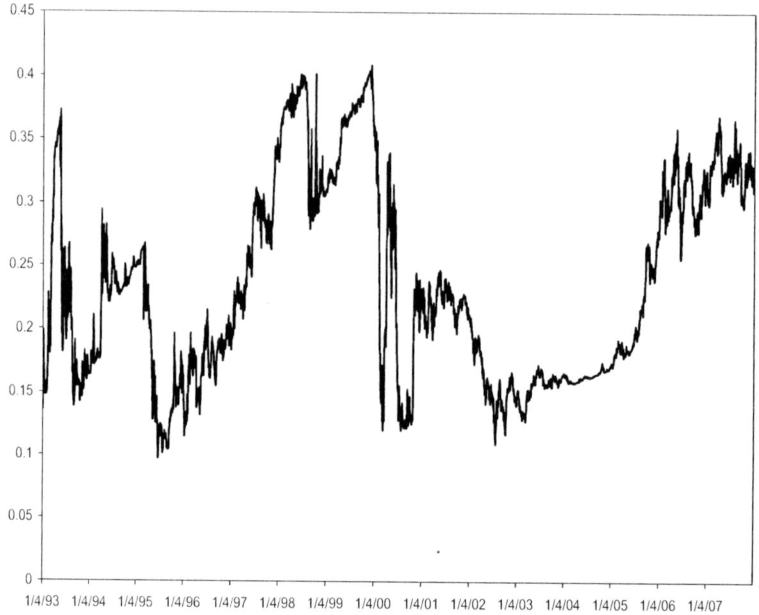

Trace Test Statistic (R, p - r = 3): Model 1

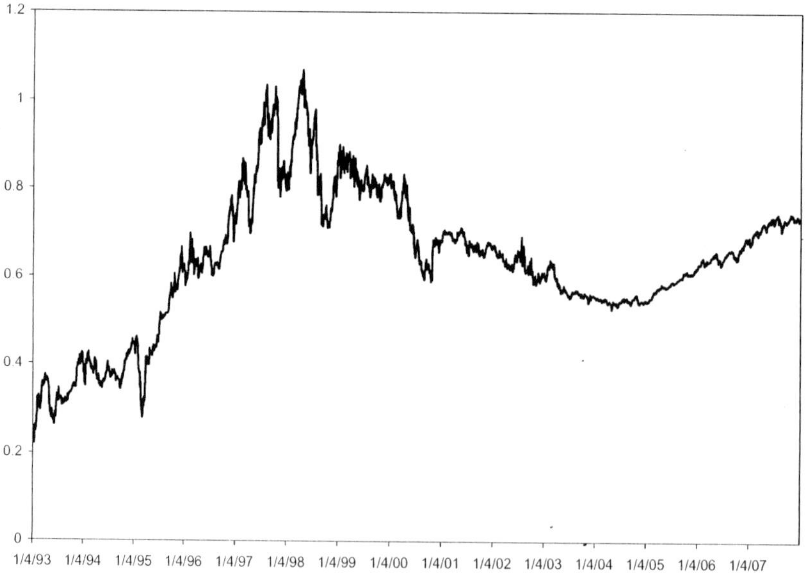

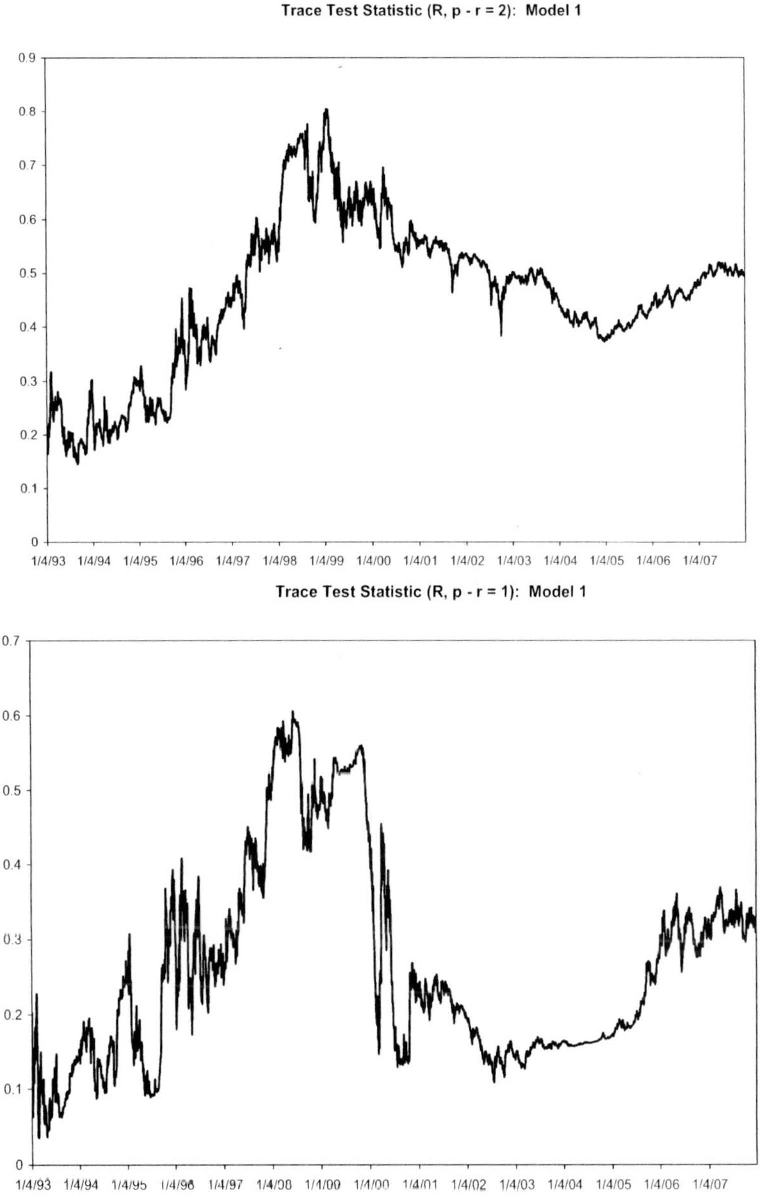

Figure 4.8. The Recursively Calculated Trace Test Statistics – Model 1.

Trace Test Statistic (X, p - r = 3): Model 2

Trace Test Statistic (X, p - r = 2): Model 2

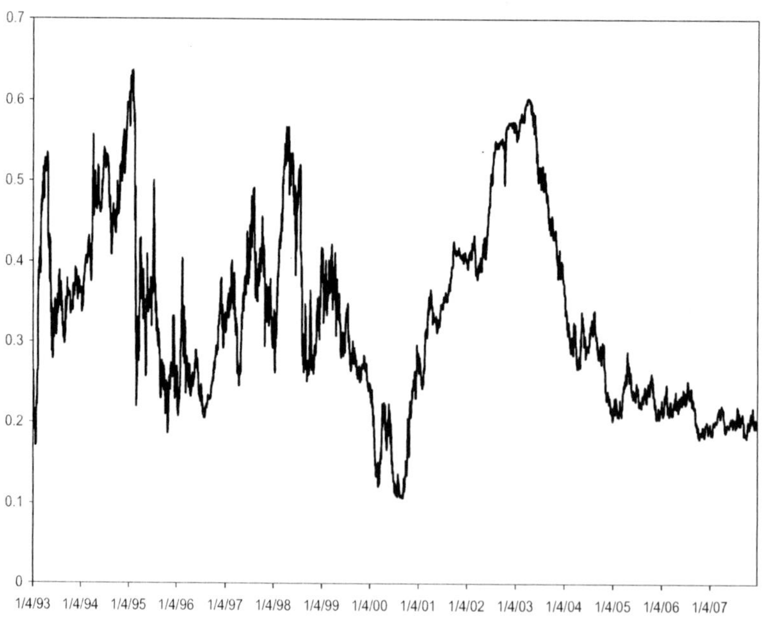

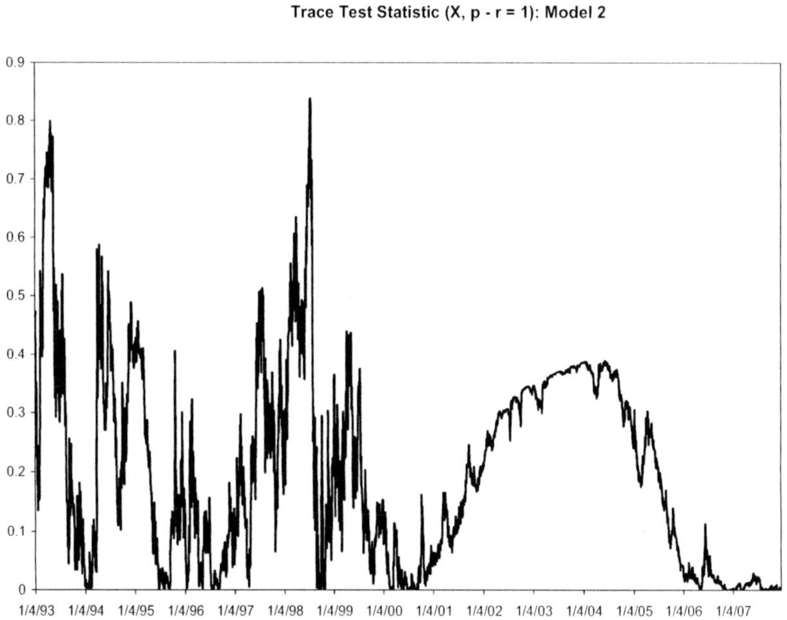

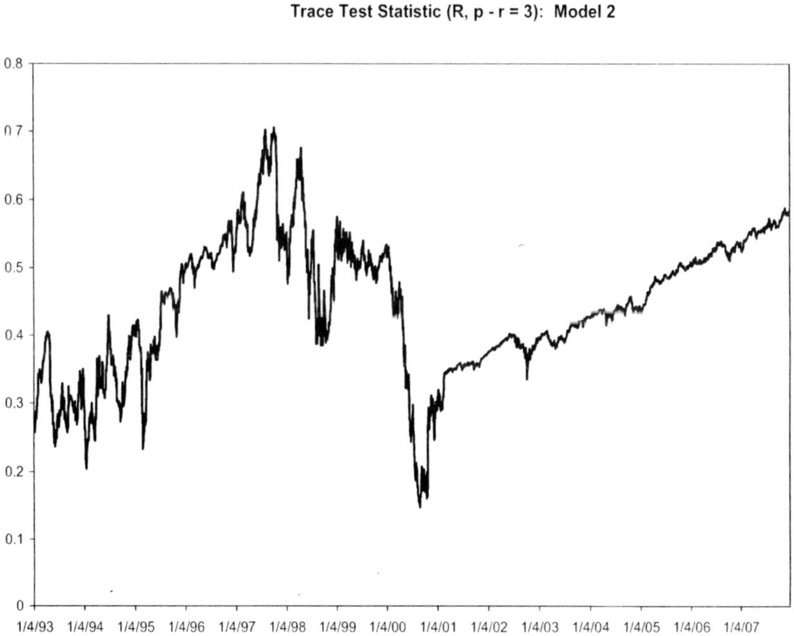

Figure 4.9. (Continued)

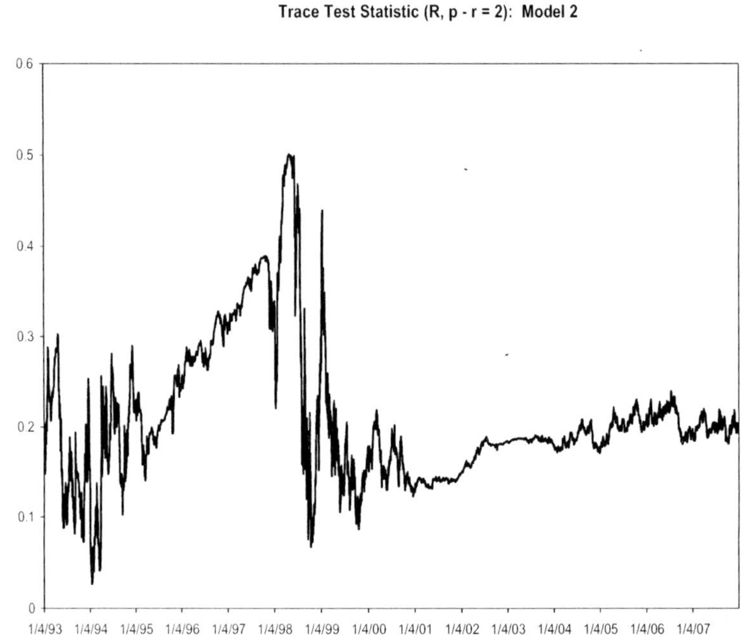

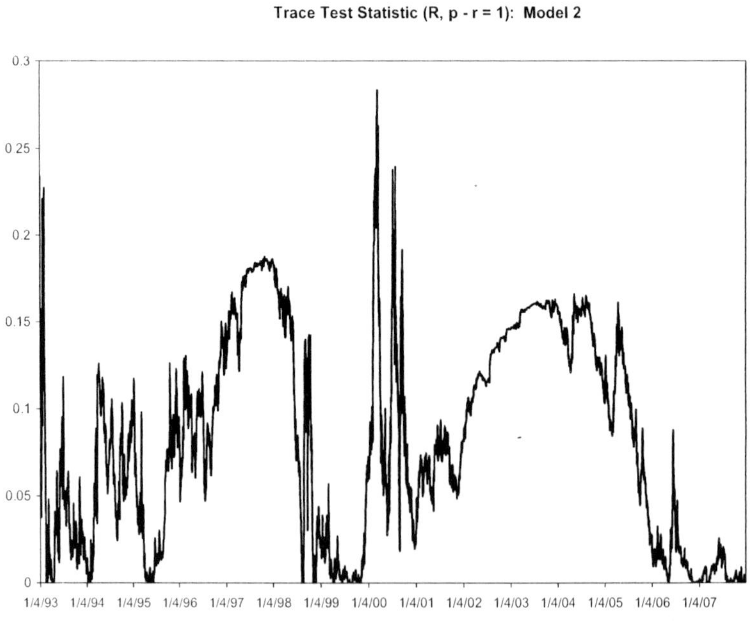

Figure 4.9. The Recursively Calculated Trace Test Statistics – Model 2.

Trace Test Statistic (X, p - r = 3): Model 3

Trace Test Statistic (X, p - r = 2): Model 3

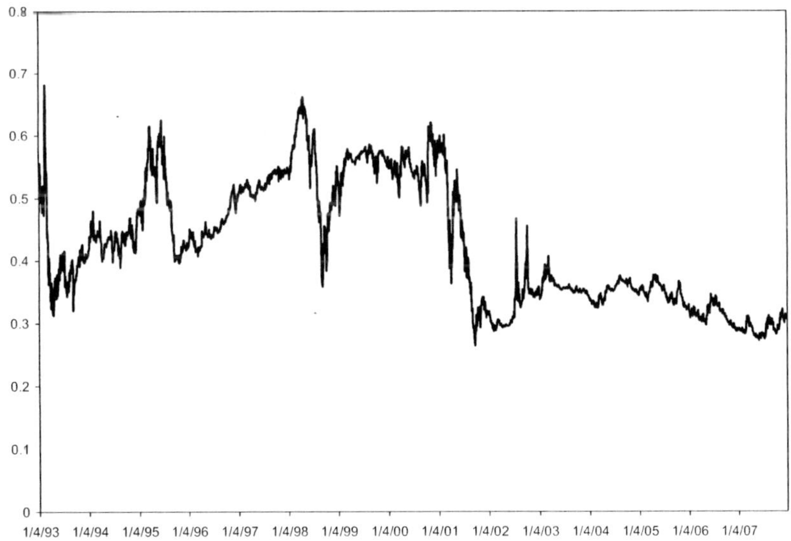

Figure 4.10. (Continued)

Trace Test Statistic (X, p - r = 1): Model 3

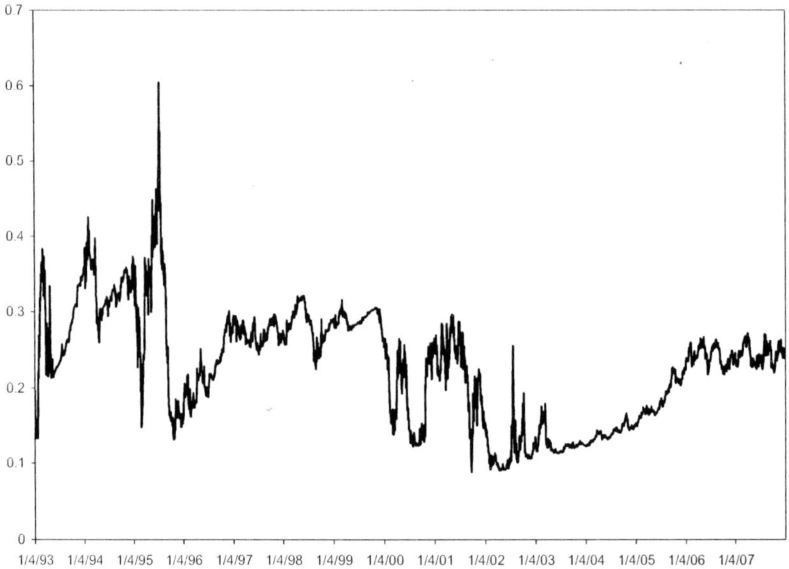

Trace Test Statistic (R, p - r = 3): Model 3

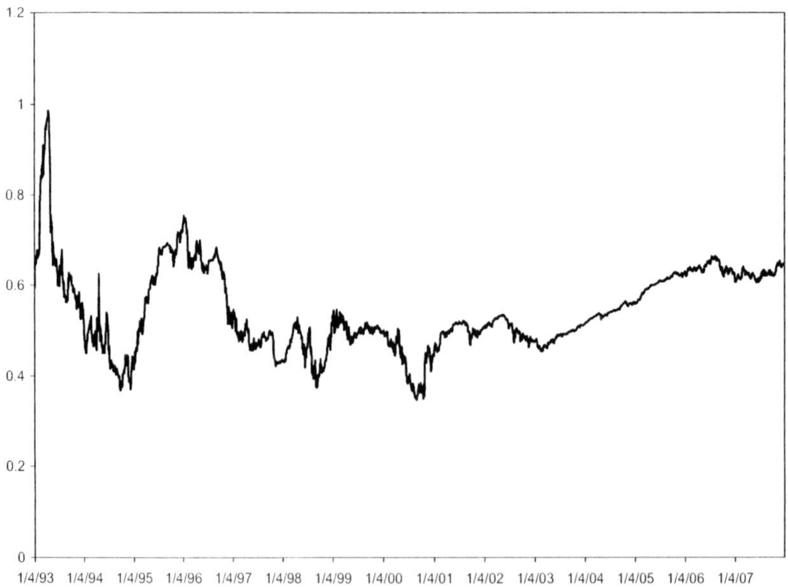

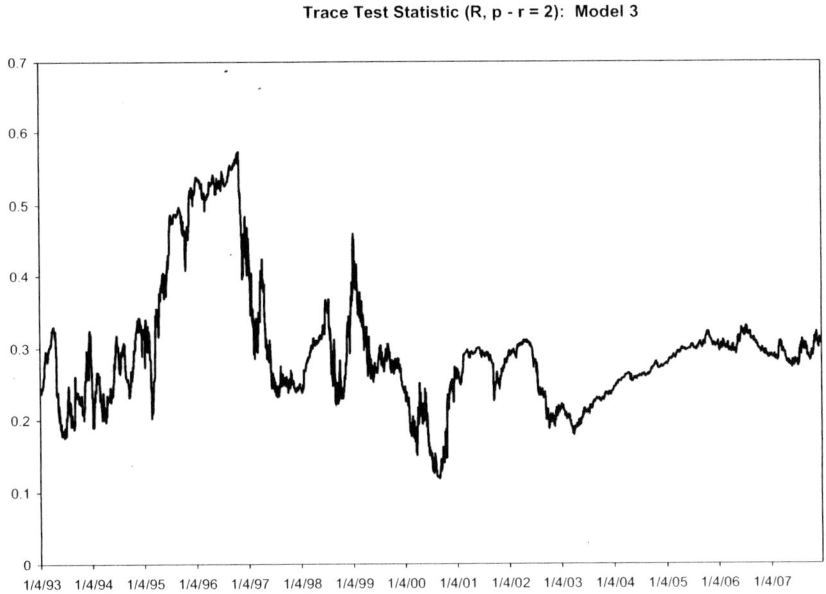

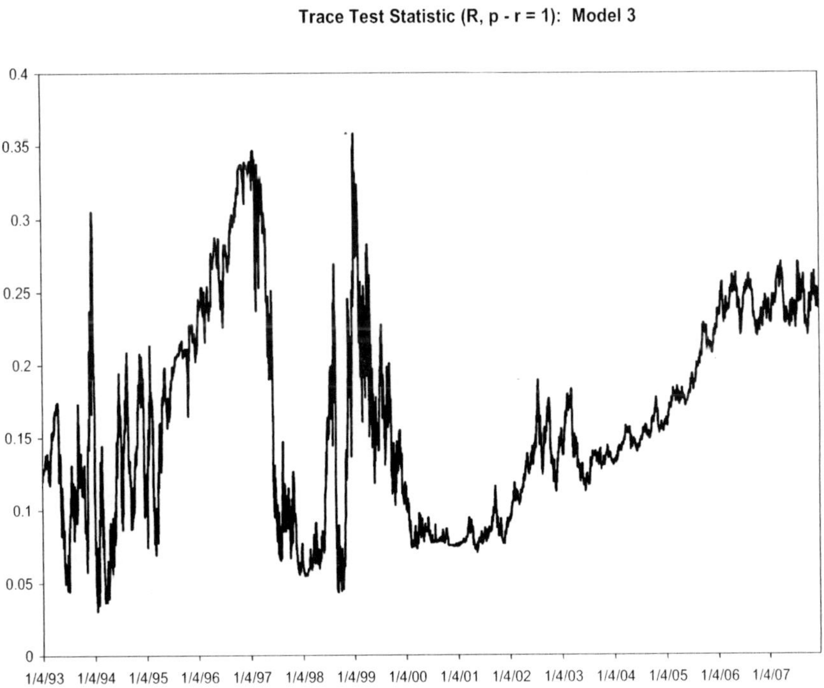

Figure 4.10. The Recursively Calculated Trace Test Statistics – Model 3.

Rangvid (2001) employs the recursive cointegration approach to analyze the process of integration among European stock markets and suggests that a larger number of cointegrating relationships provides support for the contention that European stock markets exhibited a process of convergence.

The rescaled trace statistics suggest rejection of the null hypotheses of no cointegration, if it exceeds one. In addition, the slope of the rescaled trace statistic determines the direction of co-movements between the three stock markets. An upward slope indicates rising co-movement, while a downward slope reveals declining co-movement between the three markets. In the R-representation of Models 1 and 2 (but not Model 3), we observe a strengthening of the relationship in the mid-nineties, as the three North-American markets display a movement toward cointegration. This movement, however, reverses itself at the end of the nineties. Furthermore, even when the tests statistics show a tendency to increase, they still remain below their critical values.

In sum, the hypothesis that co-movements among the three North-American equity markets increased over time does not receive support from the data, as the number of cointegrating vectors even in the most recent years has remained zero. In general, therefore, the results of the recursive forward trace tests prove congruent with the results from the traditional cointegration analysis. Therefore, we find no evidence of a common long-term trend between the three North-American equity indices, and no evidence of a possible strengthening of any such trend.

4.4. Rolling Cointegration

Pascual (2003) suggests that the recursive approach may provide misleading results, as an increasing recursive test statistic may simply reflect the increased the power of the test due to increased sample size rather than provide evidence of increased market integration. To check the robustness of the results obtained from the recursive estimation, we also employ a rolling cointegration approach. This provides additional information on the degree of market integration, using a sequence of non-overlapping time periods of equal length. We fix the length of the rolling estimation window at a 10-year interval, because cointegration is a long-run property and we need reasonably long time spans of data to detect the existence of cointegrating vectors.

Trace Test Statistic (X, p - r = 3): Model 1

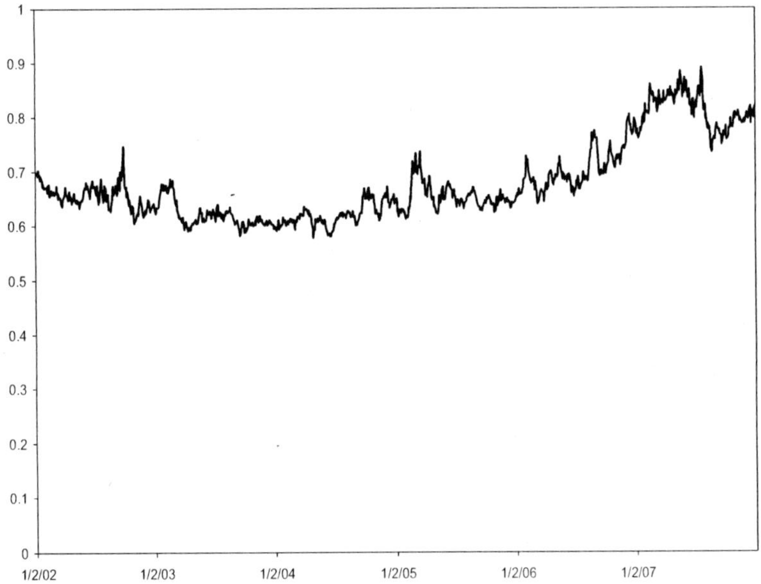

Trace Test Statistic (X, p - r = 2): Model 1

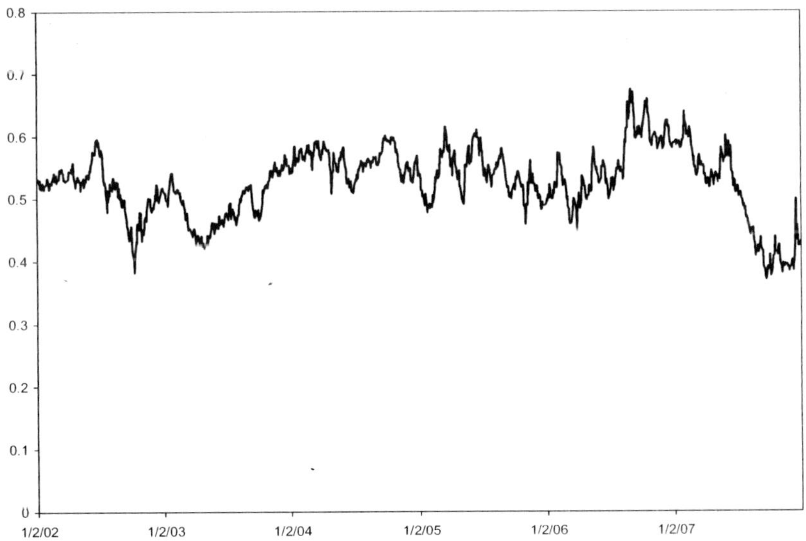

Figure 4.11. (Continued)

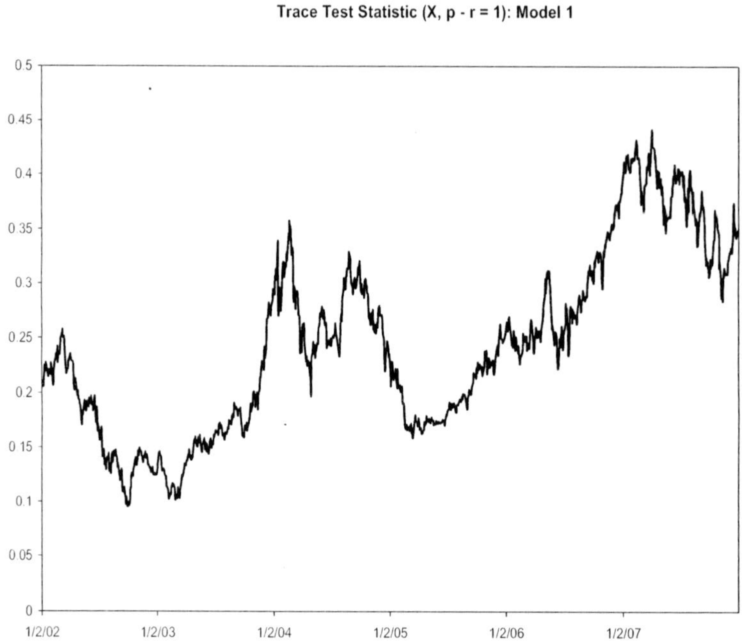

Figure 4.11. Rolling Trace Test Statistics – Model 1.

The plots of the rolling trace statistics through time show the strength of cointegrating relations (and, thus, the degree of convergence) over adjacent fixed intervals within the full sample period. The first estimation window equals January 2, 1992 to January 2, 2002, while the last estimation window equals January 2, 1998 to December 31, 2007. Figures 4.11, 4.12, and 4.13 show the rolling trace statistics, rescaled to the 5-percent critical values. These results correspond to the Johansen and Juselius (1990) Models 1, 2, and 3. Due to software limitations, we can only report the unrestricted or X-representation. The results of the rolling cointegration tests do not alter the conclusion of the recursive cointegration analysis, and also prove consistent with the findings based on the full sample cointegration analysis. Thus, based upon linear cointegration tests, the North American equity markets do not exhibit cointegration or even segmented cointegration. That is, some shared economic growth factors underlying earnings and dividends do not drive the long-run paths of the stock market prices in these markets (Crowder and Wohar, 1998). Alternatively, investors do not face fewer assets than those available in a simple count of the number of markets and, therefore, no restrictions exist on the long-run gains from diversification (Chen, Firth, and Rui, 2002).

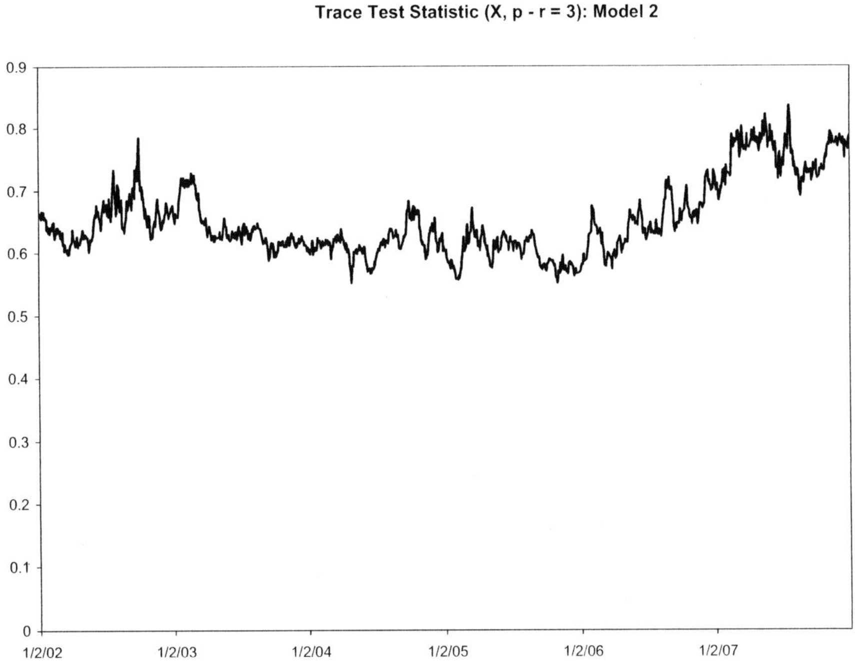

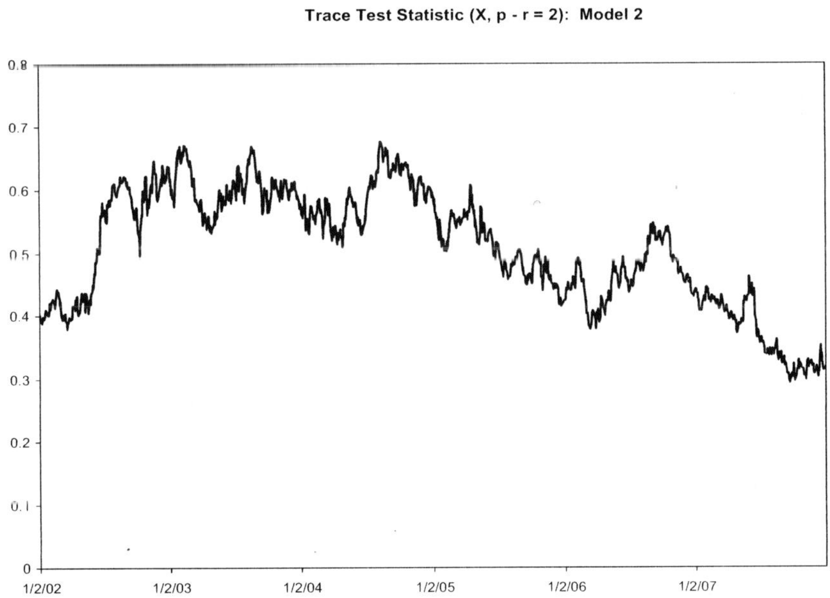

Figure 4.12. (Continued)

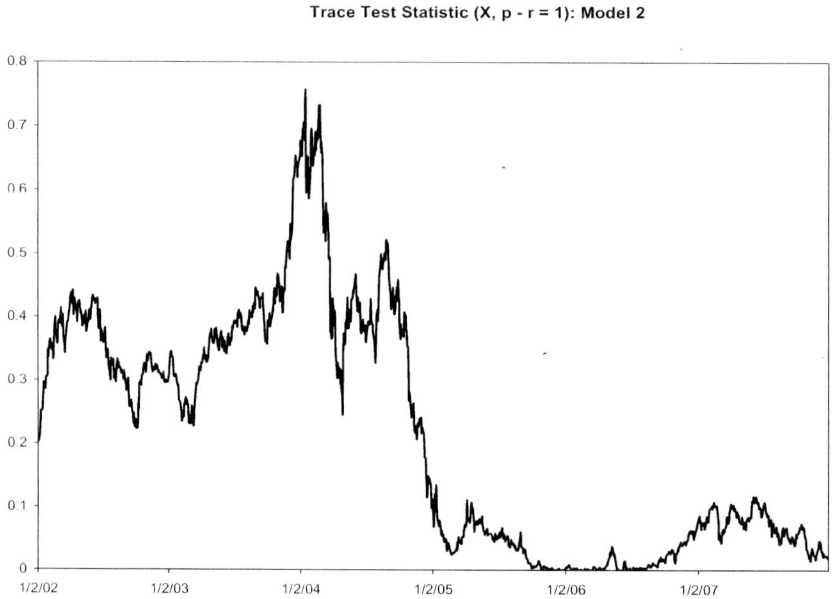

Figure 4.12. Rolling Trace Test Statistics – Model 2.

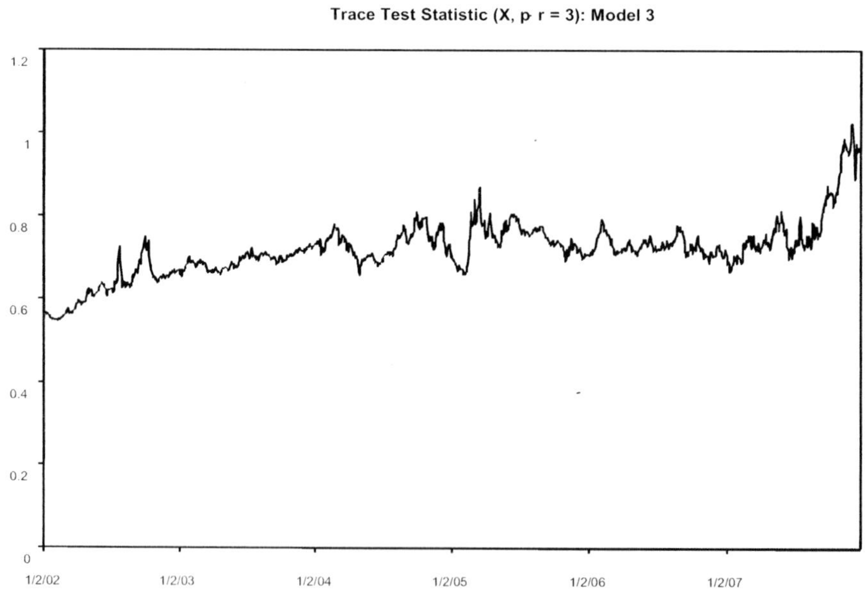

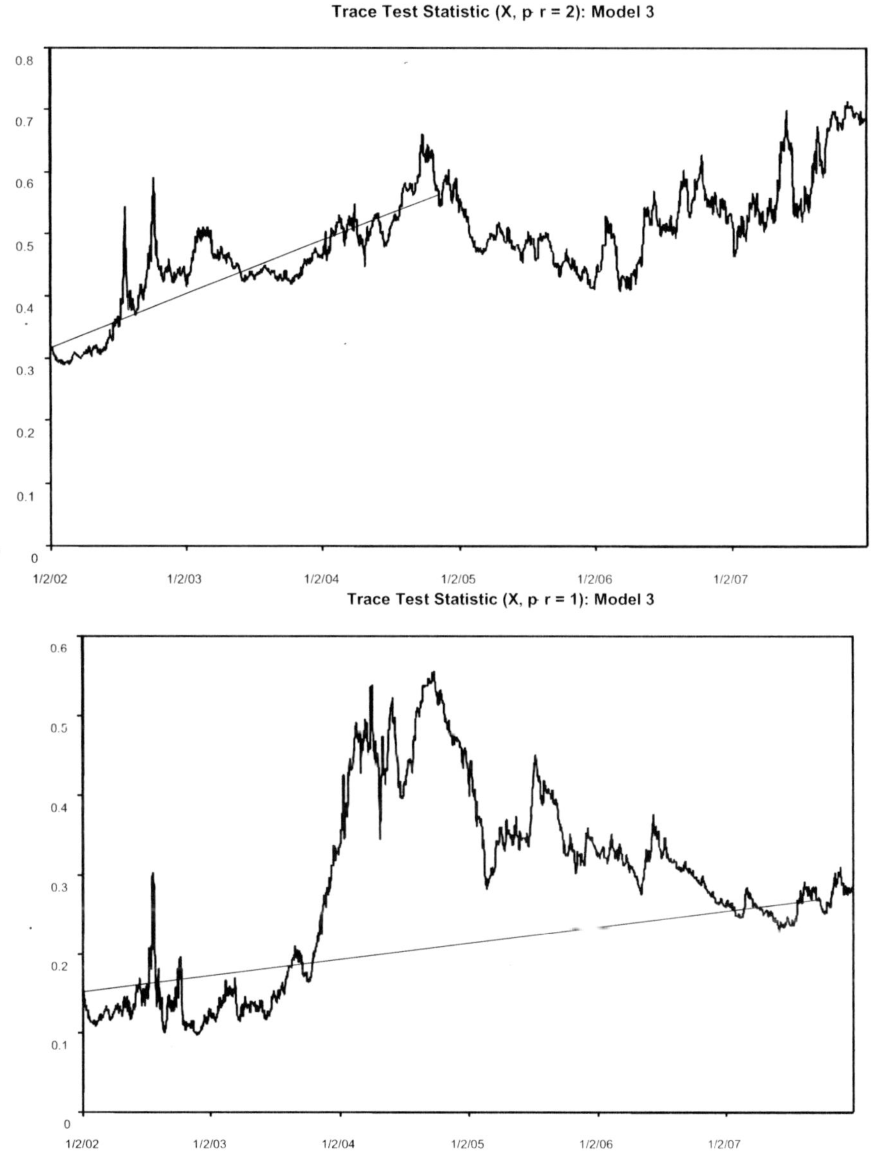

Figure 4.13. Rolling Trace Test Statistics – Model 3.

4.5. Cointegration and Structural Change

Researchers generally view equity-market integration as a smooth and gradual process, but abrupt events can affect that integration process through shifts in the mean and/or the trend of the series. As noted by Perron (1989), ignoring the issue of potential structural breaks in the data-generating process can render invalid not only unit-root test, but also cointegration tests. Conventional tests for identifying the existence of unit roots in a series, such as the ADF or the PP tests may incorrectly indicate the existence of a unit root, when, in fact, the series is stationary around a single (one-time) structural break. In this section, we discuss and apply the unit-root tests based on the Zivot and Andrews (1992) model. Then, we discuss and apply the Gregory and Hansen (1996) cointegration techniques in the presence of endogenously determined breaks. Campos, Ericson and Hendry (1996) show, using Monte-Carlo experiments, that when a shift in parameters takes place, conventional tests for cointegration may lose power and falsely signal the absence of a long-run equilibrium relationship. Gregory and Hansen (1996) argue that such testing procedures prove particularly relevant when we cannot reject the null hypothesis of no cointegration by the conventional tests.

Perron (1989) assumes that an exogenous timing of the structural break and shows that the power to reject a unit root decreases for stationarity series with an ignored structural break. Zivot and Andrews (1992) propose a variation of Perron's (1989) original test by assuming an unknown time of the structural break and develop a data-dependent algorithm to determine the break point. Following Perron's (1989) characterization of the form of structural break, Zivot and Andrews (1992) use three models to test for a unit root: a) Model A, which permits a one-time change in the level of the series; b) Model B, which allows for a one-time change in the slope of the trend, and c) Model C, which combines one-time changes in the level of the series and the slope of the trend. Zivot and Andrews (1992) test for a unit root against the alternative of a one-time structural break, using the following regressions equations that correspond to the above three models:

Model A:

$$\Delta y_t = c + \alpha y_{t-1} + \beta t + \gamma DU + \sum_{j=1}^{k} d_j \Delta y_{t-j} + \varepsilon_t \ ; \tag{4.26}$$

Table 4.15. Zivot-Andrews Unit-Root Tests, 1992 – 2007

	Model A		Model B		Model C	
	Minimum *t*-statistic	Break Date	Minimum t-statistic	Break Date	Minimum *t*-Statistic	Break Date
ln(USA)	-3.61147	02/02/2001	-2.77624	01/29/1998	-3.99400	09/05/2000
ln(CAN)	-4.89398	01/31/2001	-2.44396	10/31/1996	-4.81912	02/07/2001
ln(MEX)	-3.90830	04/19/2005	-3.92387	06/24/2003	-4.81919	05/21/2002

Note: Critical values from Zivot and Andrews (1992):
a) intercept model: 1% = -5.34; 5% = -4.80;
b) trend model: 1%= -4.93; 5% = -4.42;
c) intercept and trend model: 1% = -5.57; 5% = -5.08

Model B:

$$\Delta y_t = c + \alpha y_{t-1} + \beta t + \theta DT + \sum_{j=1}^{k} d_j \Delta y_{t-j} + \varepsilon_t \text{ ; and} \quad (4.27)$$

Model C:

$$\Delta y_t = c + \alpha y_{t-1} + \beta t + \gamma DU + \theta DT + \sum_{j=1}^{k} d_j \Delta y_{t-j} + \varepsilon_t , \quad (4.28)$$

where *DU* is a dummy variable for a mean (intercept) shift occurring at each possible break point *TB* and *DT* is a corresponding dummy variable for a trend shift, i.e., $DU = 1$ if $t > TB$ and 0 otherwise, and $DT = t - TB$ if $t > TB$ and 0 otherwise. The null hypothesis in all three models is $\alpha = 0$, which implies that the series y_t contains a unit root with a drift that excludes any structural break, while the alternative hypothesis $\alpha < 0$ implies that the series is a trend-stationary process with a one-time break occurring at an unknown point in time.

The Zivot-Andrews method regards every point as a potential break point *TB* and estimates the models sequentially for every possible *TB*. Then, from all the possible break points, the procedure selects the break point $\overline{TB}$ that minimizes the one-sided *t*-statistic for testing the hypothesis $\alpha = 0$. According to Zivot and Andrews (1992), the asymptotic distribution of the statistic diverges toward infinity at the end points of the sample. Following the Zivot and Andrews' (1992) suggestion and common convention, we choose the "trimming region" (0.15*n*,

0.85n), where n equals the sample size. We determine the optimal lag length on the basis of the Akaike information criterion (AIC) and set k equal to 12 lags in each model. Table 4.15 presents the results of the Zivot and Andrews unit-root tests and reports the minimum t-statistics and their corresponding break dates.[2]

We fail to reject the unit-root hypothesis for each of the series, which proves consistent with the results obtained from the unit-root tests without structural break. At the same time, the tests identify endogenously the date $\overline{TB}$ of the most significant structural break. In a recent study, Sen (2003) shows that a substantial loss of power occurs if the researcher uses Model A, when, in fact, the break occurs according to Model C. If Model A characterizes the break, however, but the researcher uses Model C, the loss of power proves negligible. This suggests that Model C dominates Model A. Based on these observations, we choose Model C for the analysis of the break dates. The results indicate that the break point first occurs in the US equity market, in September 2000. Six months later, in February 2001, the model detects a break in the Canadian equity market. Finally, in May 2002, the model signals a break in the Mexican market.

Figures 4.14, 4.15, and 4.16 present the recursive results of Zivot and Andrews's (1992) tests for each series, which also contains time plots of the estimated t-statistics for each possible break date. The shift in parameters detected by the Zivot and Andrews (1992) sequential tests suggests that standard tests for cointegration can lose power and falsely signal the absence of a long-run equilibrium. It is of interest, therefore, to consider the possibility of a shift in the equilibrium relations that occurs at an unknown point in time.

The residual-based tests developed by Gregory and Hansen (1996) assume a null hypothesis of no cointegration versus the alternative of cointegration with one structural break. These tests extend the Engle and Granger (1987) test, where the researcher applied a unit-root test to the residuals from an OLS regression of a cointegrating equation that directly incorporates the structural break. That is, we estimate the timing of the structural change under the alternative hypothesis rather than select a point, *a priori*. Consequently, we now consider the results for the cointegration analysis among pairs of equity markets, when we employ the Gregory and Hansen (1996) procedure.

---

[2] We use the RATS econometrics software package 7.10 to estimate the Zivot and Andrews (1992) unit-root tests. Tom Doan and the support staff at Estima, the company that develops, supports, and maintains the RATS software, provide RATS procedures to implement a variety of econometric models and statistical tests. We modified the RATS procedure file zivot.src only with respect to the dataset used.

Zivot-Andrews Unit Root Tests USA, Intercept

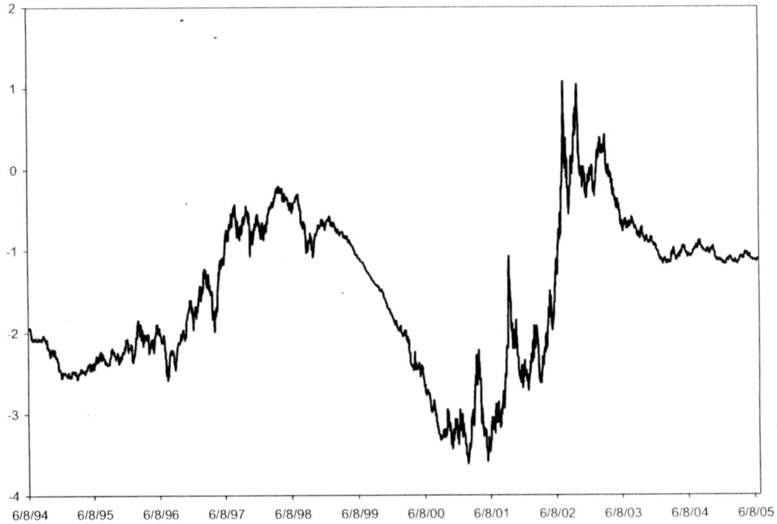

Zivot-Andrews Unit Root Tests USA, Trend

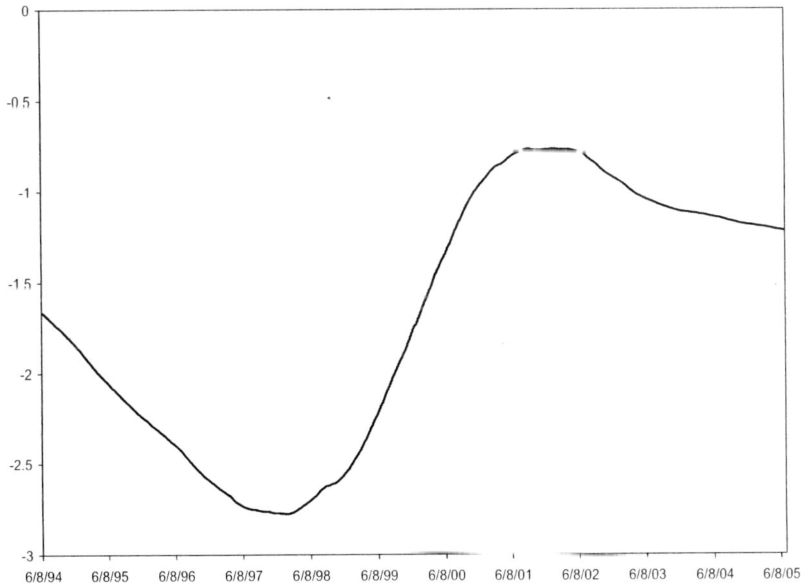

Figure 4.14. (Continued)

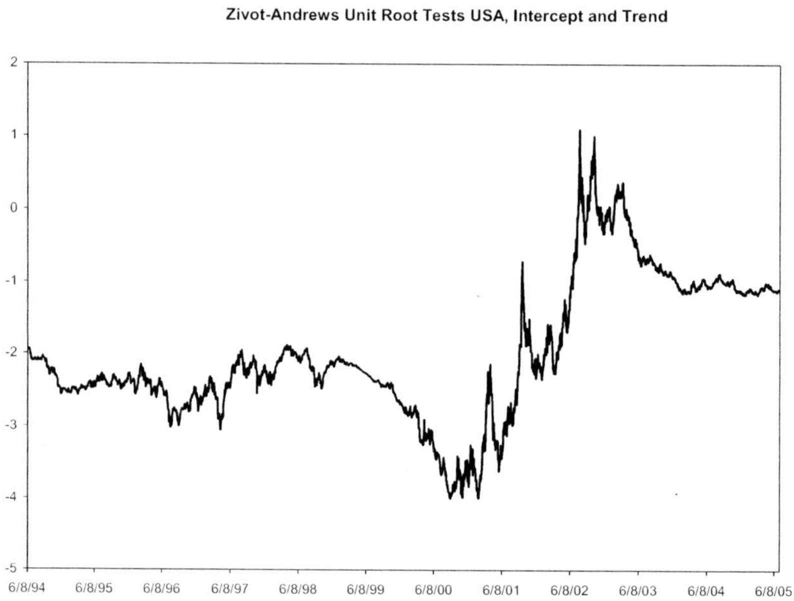

Figure 4.14. Zivot-Andrews Test Statistics for US.

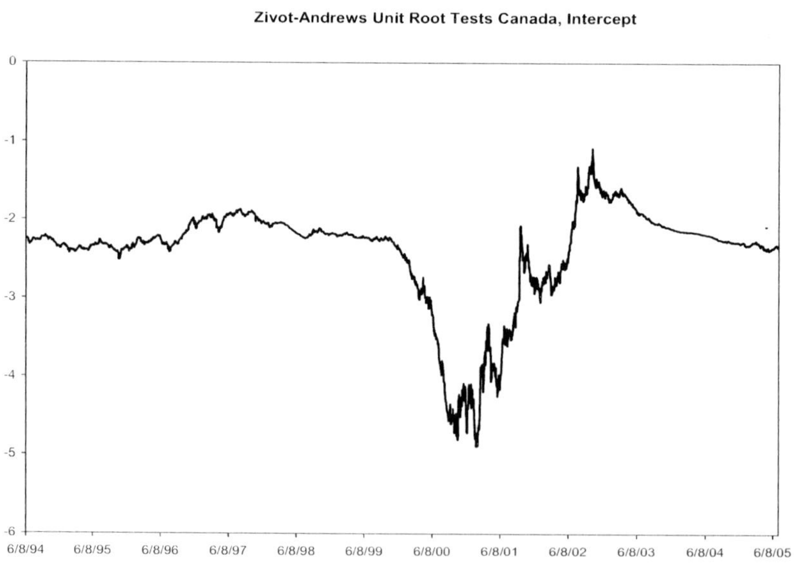

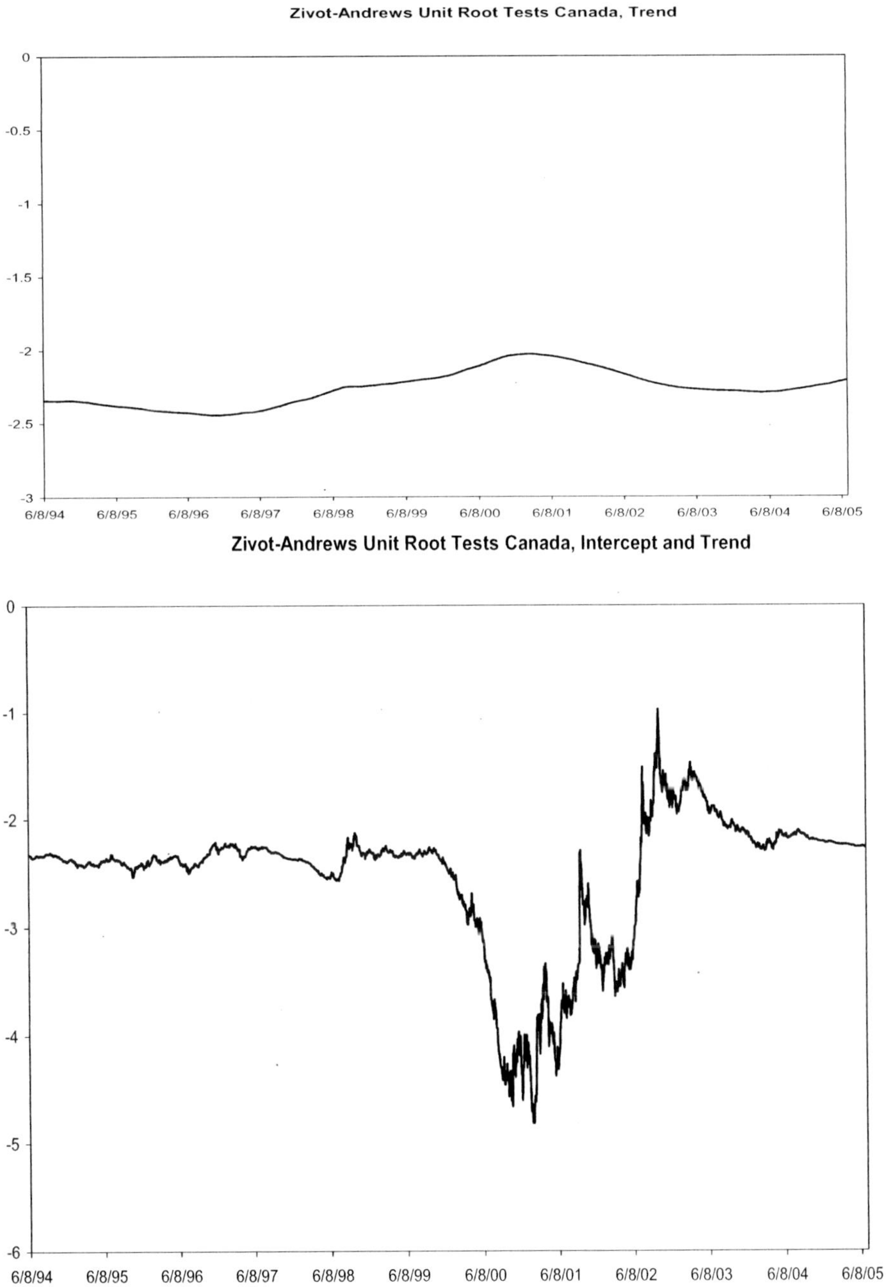

Figure 4.15. Zivot-Andrews Test Statistics for Canada.

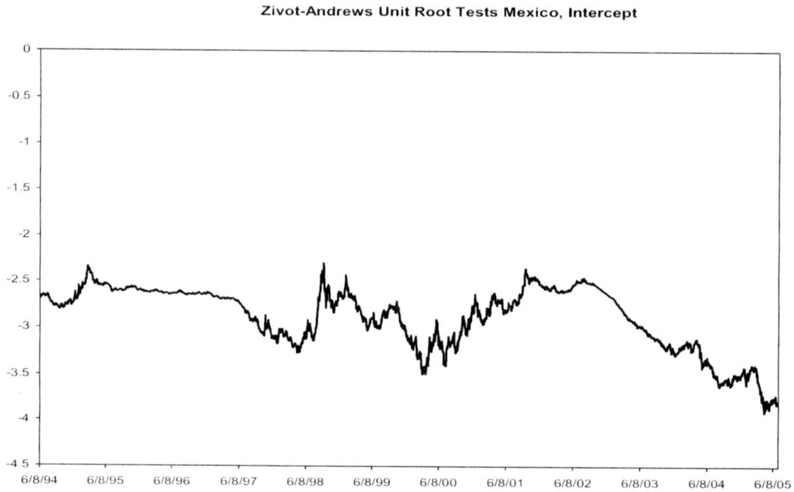
Zivot-Andrews Unit Root Tests Mexico, Intercept
0
-0.5
-1
-1.5
-2
-2.5
-3
-3.5
-4
-4.5
6/8/94
6/8/95
6/8/96
6/8/97
6/8/98
6/8/99
6/8/00
6/8/01
6/8/02
6/8/03
6/8/04
6/8/05

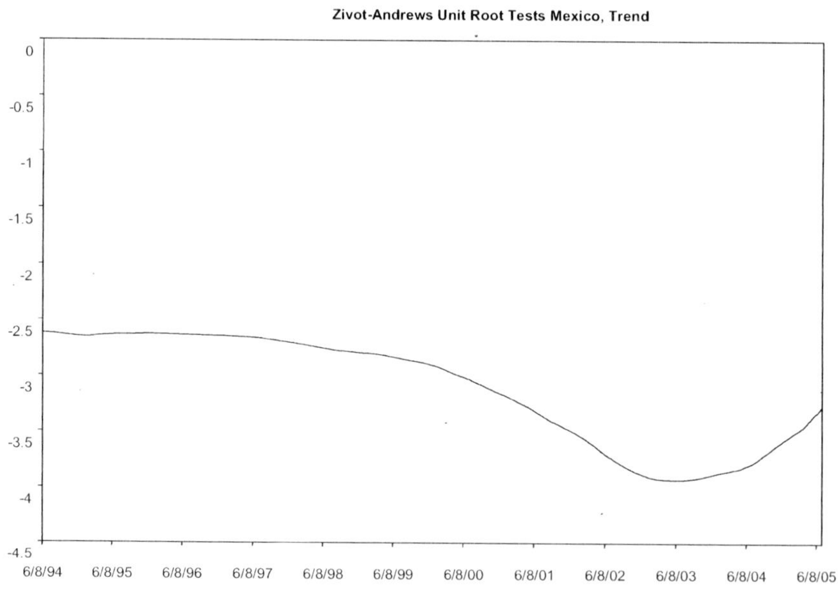
Zivot-Andrews Unit Root Tests Mexico, Trend
0
-0.5
-1
-1.5
-2
-2.5
-3
-3.5
-4
-4.5
6/8/94
6/8/95
6/8/96
6/8/97
6/8/98
6/8/99
6/8/00
6/8/01
6/8/02
6/8/03
6/8/04
6/8/05

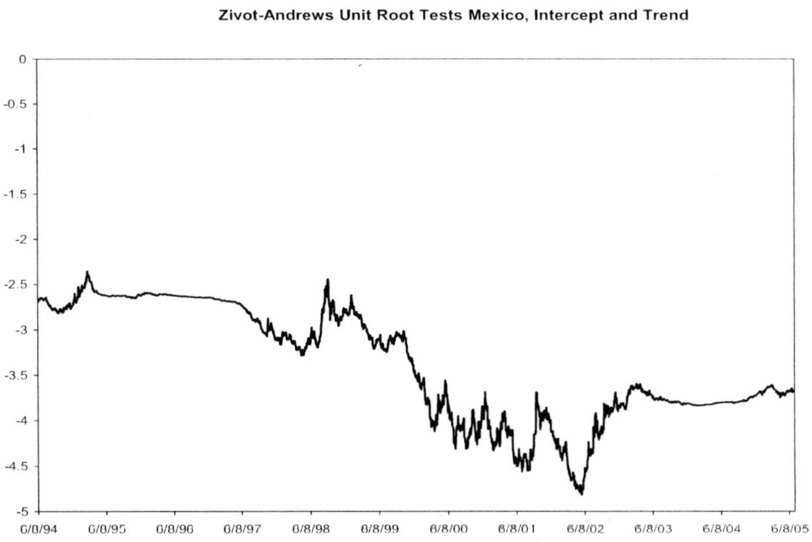

Figure 4.16. Zivot-Andrews Test Statistics for Mexico.

Gregory and Hansen (1996) suggest three alternative model specifications, accommodating parameter changes in the cointegrating vector under the alternative. The first level-shift model permits changes only in the intercept.

Model A1: Level Shift (C)

$$y_{1t} = \mu_1 + \mu_2 \xi_{t\tau} + \alpha y_{2t} + e_t, \; t = 1,2,...n. \tag{4.29}$$

where $\xi_{t\tau} = 0$, if $t \leq \text{int}[n\tau]$, and $\xi_{t\tau} = 1$, if $t > int[n\tau]$. The unknown parameter $\tau \in (0,1)$ denotes the relative timing of the break and *int* denotes the integer part. The parameter μ_1 measures the intercept before the structural break, the parameter μ_2 measures the change in intercept after the structural break and the parameter α equals the cointegrating vector.

The second model accommodates a trend in the data, while restricting the changes to shifts in the level.

Model B1: Level Shift with Trend (C/T)

$$y_{1t} = \mu_1 + \mu_2 \xi_{t\tau} + \beta t + \alpha y_{2t} + e_t, \; t = 1,2,...n. \tag{4.30}$$

The most general specification permits changes both in the intercept and in the slope of the cointegrating vector.

Model C1: Regime Shift (C/S)

$$y_{1t} = \mu_1 + \mu_2\xi_{t\tau} + \beta t + \alpha_1 y_{2t} + \alpha_2 y_{2t}\xi_{t\tau} + e_t,\ t = 1,2,...n. \qquad (4.31)$$

where α_2 measures the change in the cointegrating vector after the structural change.

We estimate Models A1, B1, and C1 sequentially with the break point in the interval $(0.15n, 0.85n)$, where n is the sample size. Table 4.16 reports the results of the Gregory and Hansen (1996) tests, where ADF* denotes the smallest value of the ADF statistics across all values of $\tau \in T$, where T=(0.15, 0.85). Figures 4.17, 4.18, and 4.19 plot the sequentially estimated ADF statistics.[3]

Table 4.16. Gregory-Hansen Cointegration Tests, 1992 – 2007

Indices	ADF*	Lags	Break date
Model A1: Level Shift			
US-Canada	-2.8681	12	4/28/2005
US-Mexico	-2.9743	12	3/25/1997
Canada-Mexico	-3.9543	2	7/30/2002
Critical values equal -5.13 for 1% and -4.61 for 5%.			
Model B1: Level Shift with Trend			
US-Canada	-3.3231	12	7/30/1997
US-Mexico	-3.8680	12	10/10/2001
Canada-Mexico	-4.6436	2	7/11/2001
Critical values equal -5.45 for 1% and -4.99 for 5%.			
Model C1: Regime Shift			
US-Canada	-3.4958	12	3/22/2000
US-Mexico	-4.1863	12	2/27/2002
Canada-Mexico	-5.1128	2	7/11/2001
Critical values equal -5.47 for 1% and -4.95 for 5%.			

Note: Critical values are taken from Gregory and Hansen (1996).

[3] We use the RATS econometrics software package 7.10 to estimate the regime shift cointegration models and resulting tests. Tom Doan and the support staff at Estima, the company that develops, supports, and maintains the RATS software, provide a replication of the results of a variety of papers using RATS procedures. They programmed the Gregory and Hansen (1996) procedure. We have modified this RATS procedure file gregoryhansen.src only with respect to the dataset used.

Gregorgy-Hansen Tests for Cointegration US and Canada, Constant

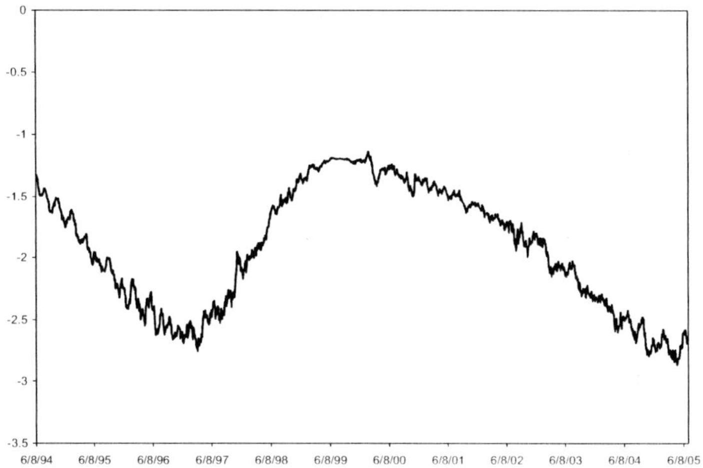

Gregorgy-Hansen Tests for Cointegration US and Canada, Trend

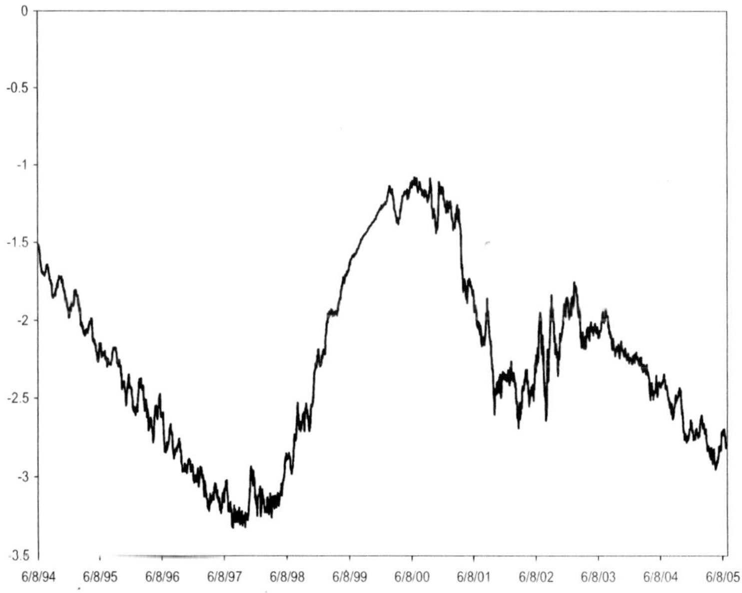

Figure 5.17. (Continued)

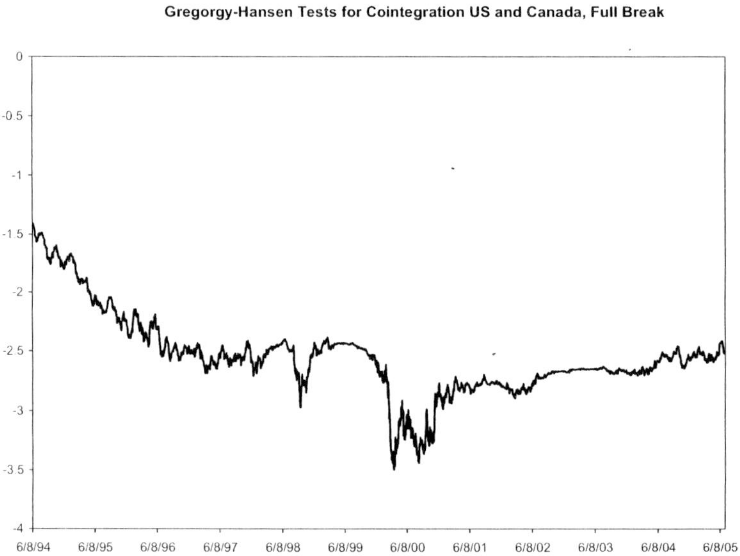

Figure 4.17. Gregory-Hansen Test Statistics for US-Canada.

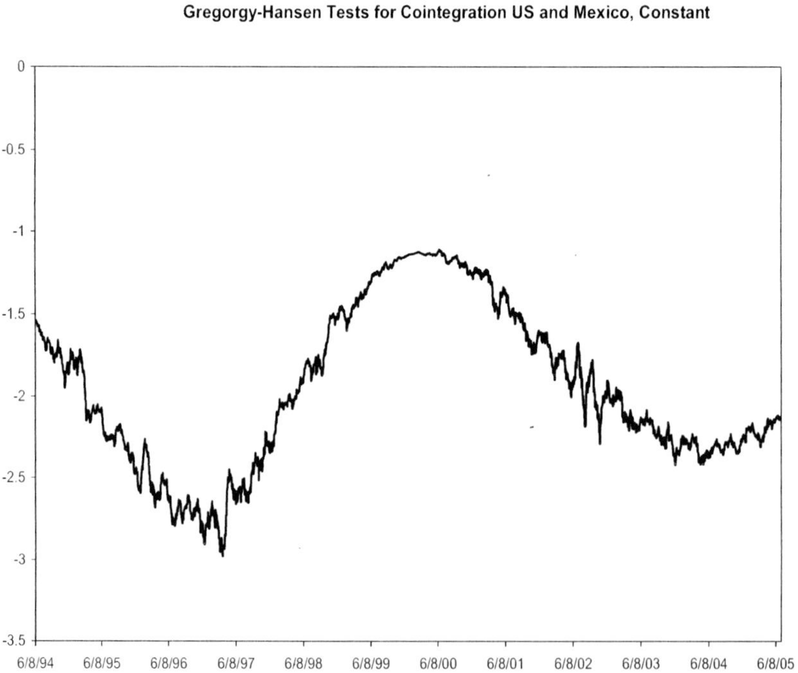

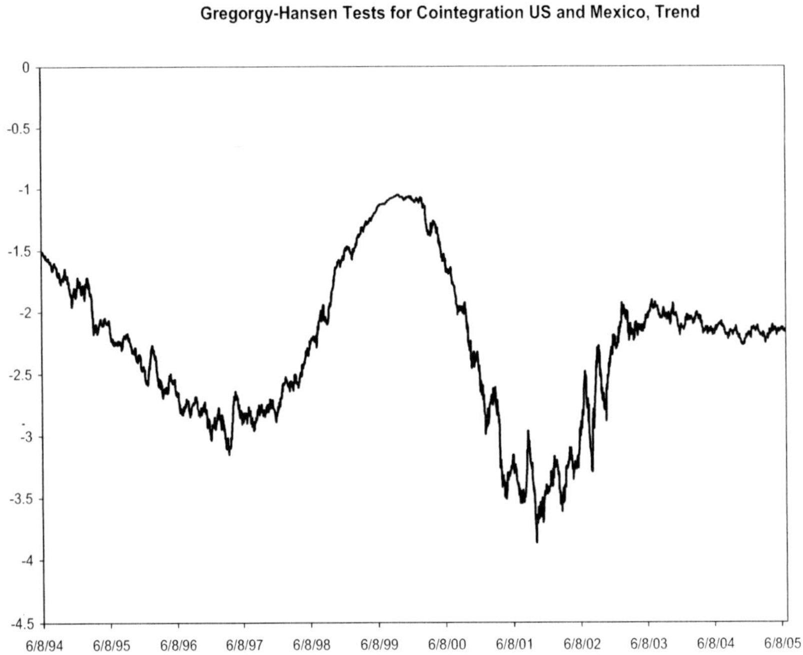

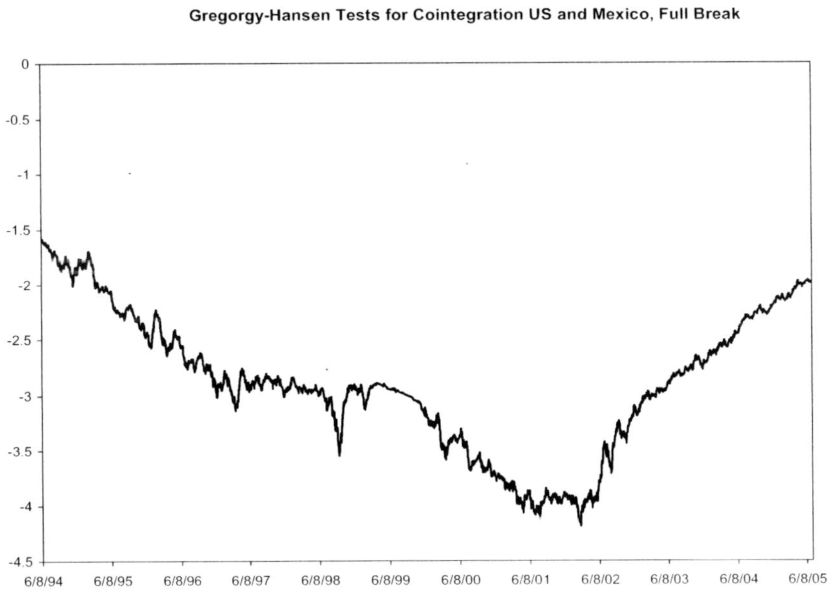

Figure 4.18. Gregory-Hansen Test Statistics for US-Mexico.

Gregorgy-Hansen Tests for Cointegration Canada and Mexico, Constant

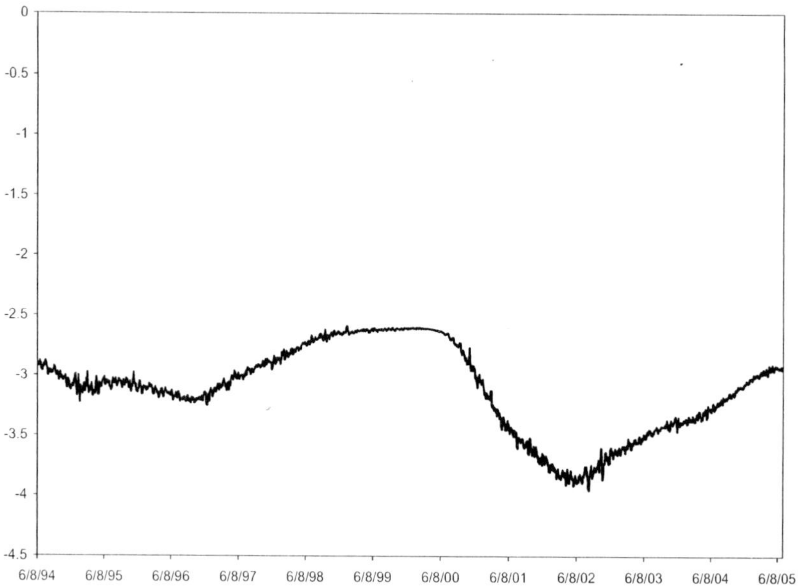

Gregorgy-Hansen Tests for Cointegration Canada and Mexico, Trend

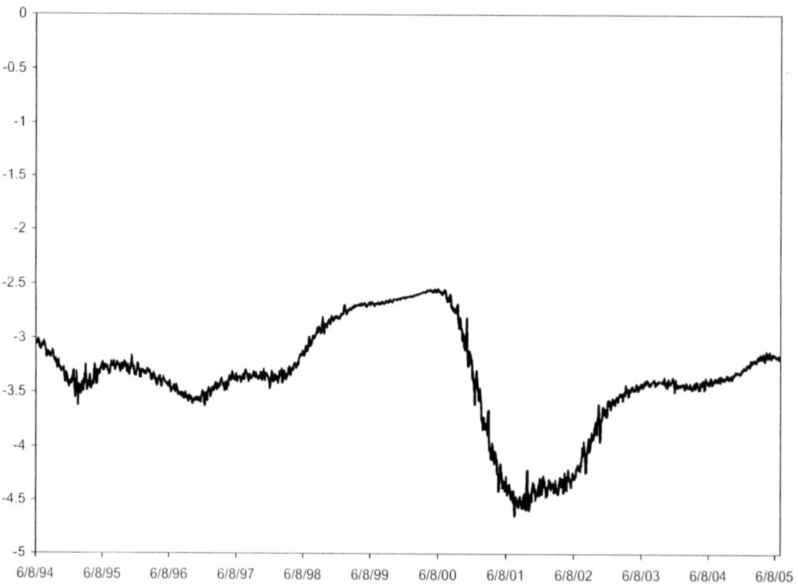

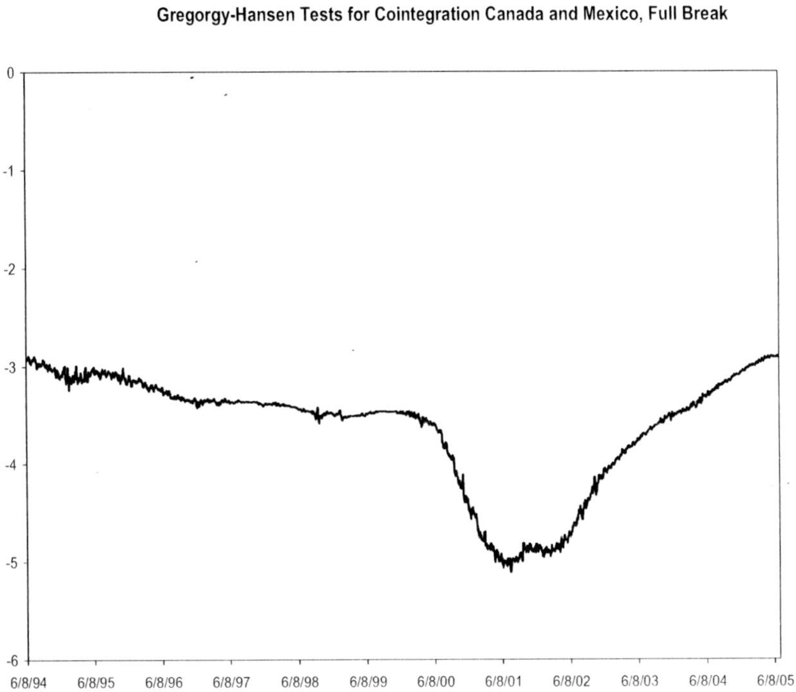

Figure 4.19. Gregory-Hansen Test Statistics for Canada-Mexico.

The pairwise results indicate that we cannot reject the null hypothesis of no cointegration in all cases at the 1-percent level. Thus, like the Johansen test results, the Gregory and Hansen results do not support a cointegrating relationship between each pair of North American equity markets. This confluence of findings also suggests that the conclusion of no cointegration in the Gregory and Hansen (1996) tests do not reflect problems associated with residual-based tests. Unlike the Johansen (1992) tests, residual-based tests impose a common-factor restriction between the variables. Kremers, Ericsson, and Dolado (1992) show that if this common-factor restriction is rejected, then the residual-based tests suffer a loss of power. Consider, for example, the bivariate system (y_t, x_t) with cointegrating vector $(1,-1)$. The error correction (EC) model estimates

$$\Delta y_t = a\Delta x_t + bw_{t-1} + \varepsilon_t, \tag{4.32}$$

where $w_t = y_t - x_t$ equals the cointegrating residual, and tests the null hypothesis of $b = 0$. Subtracting Δx_t from both sides of equation (4.32) and rearranging terms translates the EC-model-based approach into the residual-based approach:

$$\Delta(y-x)_t = b(y-x)_{t-1} + [(a-1)\Delta x_t + \varepsilon_t]. \tag{4.33}$$

That is,

$$\Delta w_t = bw_{t-1} + e_t, \tag{4.34}$$

where

$$e_t = (a-1)\Delta x_t + \varepsilon. \tag{4.35}$$

While the null hypothesis of $b = 0$ in equation (4.32) is the same as the null hypothesis of $b = 0$ in equation (4.34), the errors in the two equations differ, and equal each other only if $\Delta x_t = 0$ or $a = 1$. This means that the residual-based tests impose the restriction of equality between the short-run and long-run elasticities. If this restriction does not hold, the residual-based tests ignore this information, resulting in a loss of power. The loss of power increases, if the cointegrating relationship does not equal unity, or $(1, -\vartheta)$, which is typically the case (Campos, Ericsson, and Hendry, 1996).

4.6. Cointegration and Threshold Effects

Failure to reject the null hypothesis in a linear cointegration test does not necessarily imply that a long-run relationship does not exist. Balke and Fomby (1997) regard the presence of a non-linear adjustment process as the main cause of failure for conventional tests of cointegrating relationships. In conventional EC models, the adjustment process to the long-run equilibrium does not depend on time under a linear behavior representation. That is, the adjustment occurs at a constant rate and depends linearly on the magnitude of the deviation. Balke and Fomby (1997) indicate, however, that equilibrium relationships exist, whereby the adjustment toward equilibrium displays a non-linear behavior over a threshold parameter, and stress the possibility that the movement towards the long-run equilibrium may not occur in every time period, since economic agents experience adjustment costs (e.g., transaction costs, legal restrictions, and economic barriers). In other words, the adjustment process to long-run equilibrium experiences a discontinuity. Only when the benefits of adjustment exceed their respective costs do economic agents react to restore equilibrium. Otherwise, no adjustment occurs when deviations from equilibrium fall below a specific threshold. The adjustment process exists only when the deviations from equilibrium exceed that threshold.

From an econometric viewpoint, the residuals of the cointegrating regression are non-stationary because of a unit root (i.e., the variables are not cointegrated). Each time the threshold is crossed, however, economic agents activate the process of adjustment that ultimately results in the stationarity of the residuals of the cointegrating regression (i.e., the variables are cointegrated).

One of the most, if not the most, important statistical issue in the theory of threshold cointegration involves the testing for the presence of a threshold effect. Balke and Fomby (1997) propose several univariate tests based on Hansen (1996) and Tsay (1989), while Lo and Zivot (2001) extend Balke and Fomby's approach to a multivariate threshold cointegration model with a known cointegrating vector. Recently, Hansen and Seo (2002) consider the case of an unknown cointegrating vector and develop a Lagrange Multiplier (LM) test for the presence of a threshold effect.

Formally, let x_t equal a p-dimensional non-stationary [i.e., I(1)] time series (i.e. stock price indices), which are cointegrated with one cointegrating (p x 1) vector β . Also, let $w_t(\beta)=\beta' x_t$ equal the stationary error-correction term. We write a linear VEC model of order $q+1$ as follows:

$$\Delta x_t = A' X_{t-1}(\beta) + u_t \tag{4.36}$$

where $X'_{t-1}(\beta) = \left(1, w_{t-1}(\beta), \Delta X_{t-1}, \Delta X_{t-2}, \ldots, \Delta X_{t-q}\right)$, A is the $k \times p$ coefficient matrix, where. $k = pq+2$, and u_t is the vector martingale difference sequence with a finite covariance matrix $\Sigma = E\left(u_t u_t'\right)$. Hansen and Seo (2002) consider a two-regime threshold cointegration model, which we can view as a non-linear VEC model of order $q+1$:

$$\Delta x_t = A_1' X_{t-1}(\beta) + u_t \text{ if } w_{t-1}(\beta) \leq \gamma \text{ and} \tag{4.37}$$

$$\Delta x_t = A_2' X_{t-1}(\dot{\beta}) + u_t \text{ if } w_{t-1}(\beta) > \gamma , \tag{4.38}$$

where γ equals the threshold parameter, and A_1 and A_2 are the coefficient matrices that govern the adjustment dynamics in the first and second regimes, respectively. Hansen and Seo (2002) suggest rewriting equations (39) and (40) as follows:

$$\Delta x_t = A_1' X_{t-1} d_{1t}(\beta) + A_2' X_{t-1} d_{2t}(\beta) + u_t , \tag{4.39}$$

where

$$d_{1t}(\beta) = I(w_{t-1} \leq \gamma), \tag{4.40}$$

$$d_{2t}(\beta) = I(w_{t-1} > \gamma), \tag{4.41}$$

and $I(.)$ denotes the indicator function. The model given by equation (4.39) specifies a two-regime threshold VEC model. Values of the error correction term w_{t-1} above or below the threshold parameter γ permit the coefficients to switch between these two regimes. Hansen and Seo (2002) propose an algorithm to estimate the threshold VEC model by a quasi-ML method based on a grid search over the cointegrating vector and the threshold parameter. In detail, Hansen and Seo (2002) consider the following likelihood function under the assumption that the errors u_t are *i.i.d.* normally distributed:

$$L(A_1, A_2, \Sigma, \gamma) = -\frac{n}{2}\log|\Sigma| - \frac{1}{2}\sum_{t=1}^{n} u_t(A_1, A_2, \gamma)' \Sigma^{-1} u_t(A_1, A_2, \gamma), \tag{4.42}$$

where

$$u_t(A_1, A_2, \gamma) = \Delta X_t - A_1' X_{t-1} d_{1t}(\gamma) - A_2' X_{t-1} d_{2t}(\gamma). \tag{4.43}$$

The maximization of the likelihood function becomes computationally feasible when we concentrate out the parameters (A_1, A_2, Σ) by holding the parameters (β, γ) fixed. This generates a constrained ML estimator that is equivalent to computing the following OLS regressions:

$$\hat{A}_1(\beta,\gamma) = \left(\sum_{t=1}^{n} X_{t-1}(\beta)X_{t-1}(\beta)' d_{1t}(\beta,\gamma)\right)^{-1} \left(\sum_{t=1}^{n} X_{t-1}(\beta)\Delta X_t' d_{1t}(\beta,\gamma)\right), \tag{4.44}$$

$$\hat{A}_2(\beta,\gamma) = \left(\sum_{t=1}^{n} X_{t-1}(\beta)X_{t-1}(\beta)' d_{2t}(\beta,\gamma)\right)^{-1} \left(\sum_{t=1}^{n} X_{t-1}(\beta)\Delta X_t' d_{2t}(\beta,\gamma)\right), \tag{4.45}$$

$$\hat{u}_t = u_t\left(\hat{A}_1(\beta,\gamma), \hat{A}_2(\beta,\gamma), \beta, \gamma\right), \text{ and} \tag{4.46}$$

$$\hat{\Sigma}(\beta,\gamma) = \frac{1}{n}\sum_{t=1}^{n} \hat{u}_t(\beta,\gamma)\hat{u}_t(\beta,\gamma)'. \tag{4.47}$$

Next, we use the estimates of $\hat{A}_1(\beta,\gamma)$, $\hat{A}_2(\beta,\gamma)$, and $\hat{\Sigma}(\beta,\gamma)$ to calculate the concentrated likelihood function:

$$L(\beta,\gamma) = L\left(\beta,\gamma,\hat{A}_1(\beta,\gamma),\hat{A}_2(\beta,\gamma),\hat{\Sigma}(\beta,\gamma)\right) = -\frac{n}{2}\log\left|\hat{\Sigma}(\beta,\gamma)\right| - n \tag{4.48}$$

in the bivariate case (i.e., $p = 2$).

The ML estimator $(\hat{\beta}, \hat{\gamma})$ minimizes $\log\left|\hat{\Sigma}(\beta,\gamma)\right|$ subject to the restriction that each regime contains at least a pre-specified fraction π_0 of the total sample: That is,

$$\pi_0 \le n^{-1}\sum_{t=1}^{n} 1(w_{t-1} \le \gamma) \le 1 - \pi_0, \tag{4.49}$$

where π_0 equals a trimming parameter with values between 0.05 and 0.15 (Andrews, 1993). Since they cannot differentiate $L(\beta,\gamma)$, Hansen and Seo (2002) propose a numerical maximization method based on a grid search, starting with a consistent estimate of β obtained from the linear model (i.e., the Johansen ML estimation). The grid search procedure sets a sub-region of the parameter space for β based on the confidence interval $[\beta_L, \beta_U]$ constructed from the linear estimate $\tilde{\beta}$. Similarly, the grid search procedure also sets the sub-region of the parameter space for λ based on the interval $[\gamma_L, \gamma_U]$, where γ_L and γ_U represent the π_0 and $1-\pi_0$ percentiles of w_{t-1} based on the linear estimate $\tilde{\beta}$.

Hansen and Seo (2002) propose two supremum Lagrange Multiplier (LM) tests, following Andrews (1993) and Andrews and Ploberger (1994). They use the first test when they know the true cointegrating vector *a priori.* They denote this test as follows:

$$\text{Sup LM}^0 = \sup_{\lambda_L \le \gamma \le \gamma_U} \text{LM}(\beta_0, \gamma), \tag{4.50}$$

where β_0 equals the known value of β. They use the second test when they do not know the true cointegrating vector. We denote this test as follows:

$$\text{Sup LM} = \sup_{\lambda_L \le \gamma \le \gamma_U} \text{LM}(\tilde{\beta}, \gamma), \tag{4.51}$$

where $\tilde{\beta}$ equals the estimate of β.

Since we cannot differentiate the LM function, we evaluate it by means of a grid search. In both tests, $[\gamma_L, \gamma_U]$ equals the search region so that γ_L is the π_0 percentile of $\tilde{w}_{t-1}$, and γ_U is the $(1-\pi_0)$ percentile, with π_0 set between 0.05 and 0.15 (Andrews, 1993). Since they do not know the asymptotic distribution of the tests Hansen and Seo (2002) suggest using the fixed regressor bootstrap (Hansen, 1996) or the parametric residual bootstrap to calculate asymptotic critical values and *p*-values.

We explore the possibility that threshold cointegration provides a better empirical representation of the long-run relationships between the three North

American equity markets, using three bivariate threshold VAR model with one lag (i.e., $q = 1$).

1) The US-Mexico Model:

$$\Delta \log I_t^{US} = \mu_1 + \delta_1 w_{1,t-1} + \eta_{11} \Delta \log I_{t-1}^{US} + \eta_{12} \Delta \log I_{t-1}^{MEXICO} + u_{1t}^{US}, \quad \text{and}$$
$$\text{where } w_{1,t-1} \le \gamma_1 \tag{4.52a}$$

$$\Delta \log I_t^{MEXICO} = \mu_2 + \delta_2 w_{1,t-1} + \eta_{21} \Delta \log I_{t-1}^{US} + \eta_{22} \Delta \log I_{t-1}^{MEXICO} + u_{2t}^{MEXICO},$$
$$\text{where } w_{1,t-1} > \gamma_1, \tag{4.52b}$$

where

$$w_{1,t-1} = \log I_t^{US} - \beta_1 \log I_t^{MEXICO}. \tag{4.52c}$$

2) The US-Canada Model:

$$\Delta \log I_t^{US} = \vartheta_1 + \varphi_1 w_{2,t-1} + \xi_{11} \Delta \log I_{t-1}^{US} + \xi_{12} \Delta \log I_{t-1}^{CANADA} + u_{3t}^{US}, \quad \text{and}$$
$$\text{where } w_{2,t-1} \le \gamma_2 \tag{4.53a}$$

$$\Delta \log I_t^{CANADA} = \vartheta_2 + \varphi_2 w_{2,t-1} + \xi_{21} \Delta \log I_{t-1}^{US} + \xi_{22} \Delta \log I_{t-1}^{CANADA} + u_{4t}^{CANADA},$$
$$\text{where } w_{2,t-1} > \gamma_2, \tag{4.53b}$$

where

$$w_{2,t-1} = \log I_t^{US} - \beta_2 \log I_t^{CANADA}. \tag{4.53c}$$

3) The Mexico-Canada Model:

$$\Delta \log I_t^{MEXICO} = \upsilon_1 + \zeta_1 w_{t-1}^{3} + \theta_{11} \Delta \log I_{t-1}^{MEXICO} + \theta_{12} \Delta \log I_{t-1}^{CANADA} + u_{5t}^{MEXICO},$$
$$\text{where } w_{3,t-1} \le \gamma_3 \tag{4.54a}$$

and

$$\Delta \log I_t^{CANADA} = \upsilon_2 + \zeta_2 w_{3,t-1} + \theta_{11}\Delta \log I_{t-1}^{US} + \theta_{12}\Delta \log I_{t-1}^{CANADA} + u_{6t}^{CANADA},$$
$$\text{where } w_{3,t-1} > \gamma_3, \tag{4.54b}$$

where

$$w_{3,t-1} = \log I_t^{MEXICO} - \beta_3 \log I_t^{CANADA}. \tag{4.54c}$$

In these equations, Δ equals the first-difference operator and I_t^{US}, I_t^{MEXICO}, I_t^{CANADA} equal, respectively, the stock indices of the three North American markets.[4]

Table 4.17. Tests for Threshold Cointegration

Stock Market Indices	Sup LM^0	*p*-value
US Mexico	21.25503	0.087
US Canada	21.87041	0.092
Mexico Canada	23.05407	0.063
Stock Market Indices	**Sup LM**	***p*-value**
US Mexico	22.09937	0.079
US Canada	22.86320	0.064
Mexico Canada	22.28094	0.070

Note: Hansen and Seo (2002) propose two supremum Lagrange Multiplier (LM) tests, Sup LM^0 and Sup LM, following Andrews (1993) and Andrews and Ploberger (1994).

To assess the evidence for threshold cointegration, we calculate the Sup LM test (estimated β) and the Sup LM^0 test (β=1) as developed by Hansen and

[4] We use the RATS econometrics software package version 7.10 to estimate the threshold cointegration models and calculate the p-values for the **Sup LM** and the **Sup LM^0** tests. Tom Doan and the support staff at Estima, the company that develops, supports, and maintains the RATS software, provide a replication of the results of a variety of papers using RATS procedures. They implemented the Hansen and Seo (2002) paper with the RATS program file hansenseo.prg, which we modified only with respect to the dataset used.

Seo (2002). The tests employ heteroskedastic-robust covariance matrices, and are first-order robust to GARCH effects (Hansen and Seo, 2002). The tests point support threshold cointegration in all bivariate relationships. The evidence, however, is weak. Using q = 1, we find significant Sup LM^0 and Sup LM statistics only at the 10-percent level. Extending the lag length to 2 and 3 slightly diminishes the evidence in favor of threshold cointegration. We employ the standard residual bootstrap with 1000 repetitions to calculate the p-values for the Sup LM^0 and Sup LM tests. Table 4.17 reports the findings.

Tables 4.18, 4.19, and 4.20 report the estimated two-regime threshold VAR models, obtained by means of the Hansen and Seo (2002) approach The numbers in parenthesis represent the robust (Eicker-White) standard errors of the estimated coefficients. As Hansen and Seo (2002) observe, however, "as we have no formal distribution theory for the parameter estimates and standard errors, these should be interpreted somewhat cautiously" (p. 311). For each model, we calculate the parameter estimates by minimizing equation (4.48) over a 300×300 grid on the parameters (β_i, γ_i), $i = 1,...3$, when we estimate β_i, or over a 300 grid on the parameter γ_i, $i = 1,...3$, when β_i equals a constant of one.

For the US-Mexico model in Table 4.18, the estimated cointegrating relationship does not approximate a coefficient of unity, $w_{1,t-1} = \log I_t^{US} - 0.799 \log I_t^{MEXICO}$. For the case of the estimated β_1, the estimated threshold equals the following: $\hat{\gamma}_1 = 0.352$. Thus, the first regime occurs when $\log I_t^{US} \leq 0.799 \log I_t^{MEXICO} + 0.352$. This "typical" regime includes 94 percent of the observations. The second regime, with 6 percent of the observations, occurs when $\log I_t^{US} > 0.799 \log I_t^{MEXICO} + 0.352$, which we label, following Hansen and Seo (2002), as the relatively "extreme" regime. We uncover two periods for the "extreme" regime. The first runs from August 6, 1998 to April 27, 1999. During this period, 173 trading days exist of which 161 lie in the "extreme" regime. The second period runs from July 29, 1999 to October 5, 1999. During this period, 46 trading days exist of which 33 lie in the "extreme" regime. The equation for $\Delta \ln I_t^{US}$ exhibit statistically insignificant error correction effects and dynamics, both in the "typical" and the "extreme" regimes, while the equations for $\Delta \ln I_t^{MEXICO}$ exhibits statistically insignificant error correction effects, but significant autoregressive dynamics in the "typical" regime.

Table 4.18. Threshold VEC Model Estimates for US and Mexican Markets

Variable	Regime 1	Regime 2	Regime 1	Regime 2
	β_1 estimated		$\beta_1 = 1$	
	Equation 1 : $\Delta \ln I_t^{US}$			
constant	0.00032	0.00519	0.00064	-0.00983
	(0.00018)	(0.00689)	(0.00059)	(0.02209)
$w_{1,t-1}$	0.00003	-0.01031	0.000166	-0.00857
	(0.00044)	(0.01621)	(0.00030)	(0.01836)
$\Delta \ln I_{t-1}^{US}$	-0.02352	0.05205	-0.022313	0.01231
	(0.02598)	(0.12178)	(0.02578)	(0.12520)
$\Delta \ln I_{t-1}^{MEXICO}$	-0.00036	-0.08913	-0.000226	-0.07267
	(0.01336)	(0.06310)	(0.01397)	(0.05019)
	Equation 2: $\Delta \ln I_t^{MEXICO}$			
constant	0.00061	-0.00185	0.00043	0.04897
	(0.00031)	(0.01365)	(0.00104)	(0.04772)
$w_{1,t-1}$	-0.00018	0.00857	-0.000119	0.03981
	(0.00073)	(0.03257)	(0.00050)	(0.03969)
$\Delta \ln I_{t-1}^{US}$	0.01380	-0.00284	0.014252	-0.05011
	(0.03721)	(0.19973)	(0.03648)	(0.22548)
$\Delta \ln I_{t-1}^{MEXICO}$	0.10603	0.00191	0.09913	0.06900
	(0.03155)	(0.09759)	(0.03129)	(0.09853)
$\hat{\beta}_1$	0.799		1.000	
$\hat{\gamma}_1$	0.352		-1.268	

Note: The first two columns of estimates estimate the value of β_1 while the second two columns impose a value of one for β_1. The numbers in parenthesis represent the robust (Eicker-White) standard errors of the estimated coefficients. The parameter γ equals the threshold parameter.

For the US-Canada model in Table 4.19, the estimated cointegrating relationship approximates that for the US-Mexico model and differs from one, $w_{2,t-1} = \log I_t^{US} - 0.777 \log I_t^{CANADA}$. For the case of the estimated β_2, the estimated threshold equals the following: $\hat{\gamma}_2 = 0.288$. Thus the first regime occurs when $\log I_t^{US} \leq 0.777 \log I_t^{CANADA} + 0.288$. This "typical" regime comprises 95 percent of the sample observations. Conversely, the second regime occurs when $\log I_t^{US} > 0.777 \log I_t^{CANADA} + 0.288$.

Table 4.19. Threshold VEC Model Estimates for the US and Canadian Equity Markets

Variable	Regime 1	Regime 2	Regime 1	Regime 2
	β_2 estimated		β_2=1	
	Equation 1: $\Delta \ln I_t^{US}$			
constant	0.00026	0.02892	-0.00042	-0.04582
	(0.00023)	(0.01677)	(0.00316)	(0.07703)
$w_{2,t-1}$	-0.00098	-0.09083	-0.00037	-0.02795
	(0.00109)	(0.05296)	(0.00150)	(0.04659)
$\Delta \ln I_{t-1}^{US}$	-0.01309	-0.04992	-0.01292	-0.08804
	(0.03133)	(0.09509)	(0.03132)	(0.09706)
$\Delta \ln I_{t-1}^{CANADA}$	-0.01852	0.04347	-0.02080	0.12090
	(0.03256)	(0.11690)	(0.03238)	(0.13043)
	Equation 2: $\Delta \ln I_t^{CANADA}$			
constant	0.00027	0.00797	0.00085	0.01873
	(0.00022)	(0.01361)	(0.00304)	(0.06144)
$w_{2,t-1}$	-0.00024	-0.02197	0.00027	0.01082
	(0.00107)	(0.04338)	(0.00145)	(0.03710)
$\Delta \ln I_{t-1}^{US}$	0.07827	0.11650	0.07851	0.08759
	(0.02615)	(0.07189)	(0.02612)	(0.07272)
$\Delta \ln I_{t-1}^{CANADA}$	0.02250	0.02045	0.01984	0.10026
	(0.03027)	(0.09465)	(0.03011)	(0.10148)
$\hat{\beta}_2$	0.777		1.000	
$\hat{\gamma}_2$	0.288		-1.680	

Note: See Table 4.18. The first two columns of estimates estimate the value of β_2 while the second two columns impose a value of one for β_2.

Table 4.20. Threshold VEC Model Estimates for Mexican and Canadian Equity Markets

Variable	Regime 1	Regime 2	Regime 1	Regime 2
	β_3 estimated		$\beta_3 = 1$	
		Equation 1: $\Delta \ln I_t^{MEXICO}$		
constant	0.00080	0.04866	0.00079	0.05717
	(0.00028)	(0.03340)	(0.00029)	0.03158
$w_{3,t-1}$	0.00021	-0.05864	0.00015	-0.07230
	(0.00067)	(0.04024)	(0.00067)	(0.04003)
$\Delta \ln I_{t-1}^{MEXICO}$	0.10120	0.09178	0.10116	0.09668
	(0.02943)	(0.11049)	(0.02942)	(0.11122)
$\Delta \ln I_{t-1}^{CANADA}$	-0.00802	-0.17723	-0.00860	-0.17181
	(0.04431)	(0.18615)	(0.04429)	(0.18767)
		Equation 2: $\Delta \ln I_t^{CANADA}$		
constant	0.00039	0.00334	0.00038	0.01221
	(0.00017)	(0.02375)	(0.00018)	(0.02261)
$w_{3,t-1}$	0.00031	-0.00352	0.00026	-0.01478
	(0.00032)	(0.02876)	(0.00032)	(0.02882)
$\Delta \ln I_{t-1}^{MEXICO}$	0.01008	0.02474	0.01012	0.02551
	(0.01285)	(0.08004)	(0.01284)	(0.08063)
$\Delta \ln I_{t-1}^{CANADA}$	0.08498	-0.11466	0.08434	-0.10623
	(0.02567)	(0.12763)	(0.02566)	(0.12899)
$\hat{\beta}_3$	0.996		1.000	
$\hat{\gamma}_3$	0.791		0.753	

Note: See Table 4.18. The first two columns of estimates estimate the value of β_3 while the second two columns impose a value of one for β_3.

This "extreme" regime includes 5 percent of the sample observations. Only one period exists for the "extreme" regime, running from December 23, 1998 to December 6, 1999 or 299 days of trading with 203 days in the "extreme" regime.

The equations for both $\Delta \ln I_t^{US}$ and $\Delta \ln I_t^{CANADA}$ exhibit statistically insignificant error correction effects in both the "typical" and "extreme" regimes. The equations for $\Delta \ln I_t^{US}$ also display insignificant dynamics. Conversely, the equations for $\Delta \ln I_t^{CANADA}$ show significant cross-dynamics, but only in the "typical" regime. The important finding, however, is that the "extreme" regime from the US-Mexico model coincides approximately with the "extreme" regime from the US-Canada model, suggesting that the US stock market provides the driving force behind these "extreme" regimes.

For the Mexico-Canada model in Table 4.20, the estimated cointegrating relationship approximates one, $w_{3,t-1} = \log I_t^{MEXICO} - 0.996 \log I_t^{CANADA}$. Consequently, as we expect, the results for the case of estimated β_3 are very similar to those that impose the unit coefficient. For the case of estimated β_3, the estimated threshold equals the following: $\hat{\gamma}_3 = 0.791$. The first regime occurs when $\log I_t^{MEXICO} \leq 0.996 \log I_t^{CANADA} + 0.791$. This "typical" regime encompasses 95 percent of the sample observations. The second regime occurs when $\log I_t^{MEXICO} > 0.996 \log I_t^{CANADA} + 0.791$. This "extreme" regime contains 5 percent of the sample observations. This period extends from February 2, 2007 to December 31, 2007, comprising 217 trading days with 192 days in the "extreme" regime.

The equations for both $\Delta \ln I_t^{MEXICO}$ and $\Delta \ln I_t^{CANADA}$ exhibits statistically insignificant error correction effects, but statistically significant autoregressive dynamics in the "typical" regime.

In conclusion, we note that error correction effects prove unimportant in all cases. Although we reject the hypothesis of linear cointegration in all cases at the 10% level, we find evidence that in the threshold framework, error correction effects are not significant.

Chapter 5

GENERALIZED IMPULSE-RESPONSE FUNCTIONS

The finding that no long-term equilibrium relationship exists between the three North-American markets does not necessarily imply that no relationship exists between these markets. We examine the short-run relationship between the three stock markets returns in this Chapter by applying the generalized impulse-response analysis introduced by Koop et al. (1996) and Pesaran and Shin (1988). Impulse-response functions can provide insights into how significantly shocks in a particular market may affect other markets though dynamic interactions among markets. The generalized impulse-response functions, however, differ from the traditional, orthogonalized impulse-response analysis, such as the one based on Choleski factorization for the orthogonalization of VAR innovations. That is, the generalized approach proves invariant to the ordering of variables in the VAR system, and hence yields results that do not depend on the ordering.

We can express the VAR model of daily stock market returns in standard form as follows:

$$R_t = C + \sum_{s=1}^{p} B_s R_{t-s} + \varepsilon_t, \; t = 1, 2, \ldots, T, \tag{5.1}$$

where R_t equals a column vector of daily returns on the market indices at time t, C equals the column vector of constant terms, B_s equal matrices of coefficients such that the ith, j^{th} component of B_s measures the effect of a change in the jth

market on the ith market after s periods and ε_t equals a column vector of innovations such that $E(\varepsilon_{it})=0$, $E(\varepsilon_{it}^2)=\sigma_{ij}$, and $E(\varepsilon_{is}\varepsilon_{jt})=0$ for $s \neq t$. Equation (4.12) assumes a return generating process, where the return of each capital market depends on a constant term, its own lagged returns, the lagged returns of other capital markets, plus a serially uncorrelated and potentially contemporaneously correlated error term, ε_{it}. The return of a market incorporates not only its own past information, but also the past information of other markets. We can transform the VAR system in equation (5.1) into an infinite moving average representation as follows:

$$R_t = \sum_{s=0}^{\infty} \Phi_s \varepsilon_{t-s}, \quad t = 1, 2, \ldots, T, \tag{5.2}$$

where Φ_s equals a matrix of moving average coefficients obtained recursively from B_s in equation (5.1). In equation (5.2), the return of a market depends on its own past shocks plus the shocks from other markets. The ith, j^{th} component of Φ_s shows the response of the ith market in s periods after a unit random shock in the jth market.

Pesaran and Shin (1998) show that the generalized impulse-response function equals the following:

$$\psi_j^g(p) = \sigma_{jj}^{-1/2} \Phi_p \Sigma e_j, p = 0, 1, 2, \ldots, s \tag{5.3}$$

where σ_{jj} equals the jth, j^{th} element in the variance-covariance matrix Σ and e_j equals a (n x 1) vector with one as its jth element and zero elsewhere.[1]

Figure 5.1 presents the estimated generalized impulse responses (along with two standard deviation bands) and Tables 5.1, 5.2, and 5.3 provide the numbers (standard errors in parenthesis).[2] Some notable findings emerge. First, the

---

[1] This differs from the more traditional impulse-response function $\psi_j^o(p) = \Phi_p P e_j$, $p = 0,1,2, \ldots$, which occurs using the Choleski decomposition $PP' = \Sigma$, where P equals an (n x n) lower triangular matrix.

[2] We calculate confidence bands using Monte Carlo integration techniques, since impulse responses prove highly non-linear functions of the estimated parameters. We set the number of Monte Carlo repetitions to 1,000.

responses exhibit large magnitudes, using the conventional definition of significant responses as those that exceed 0.20 unit standard deviations (Dekker et al., 2001; Yang et al., 2003; Masih and Masih, 2001).

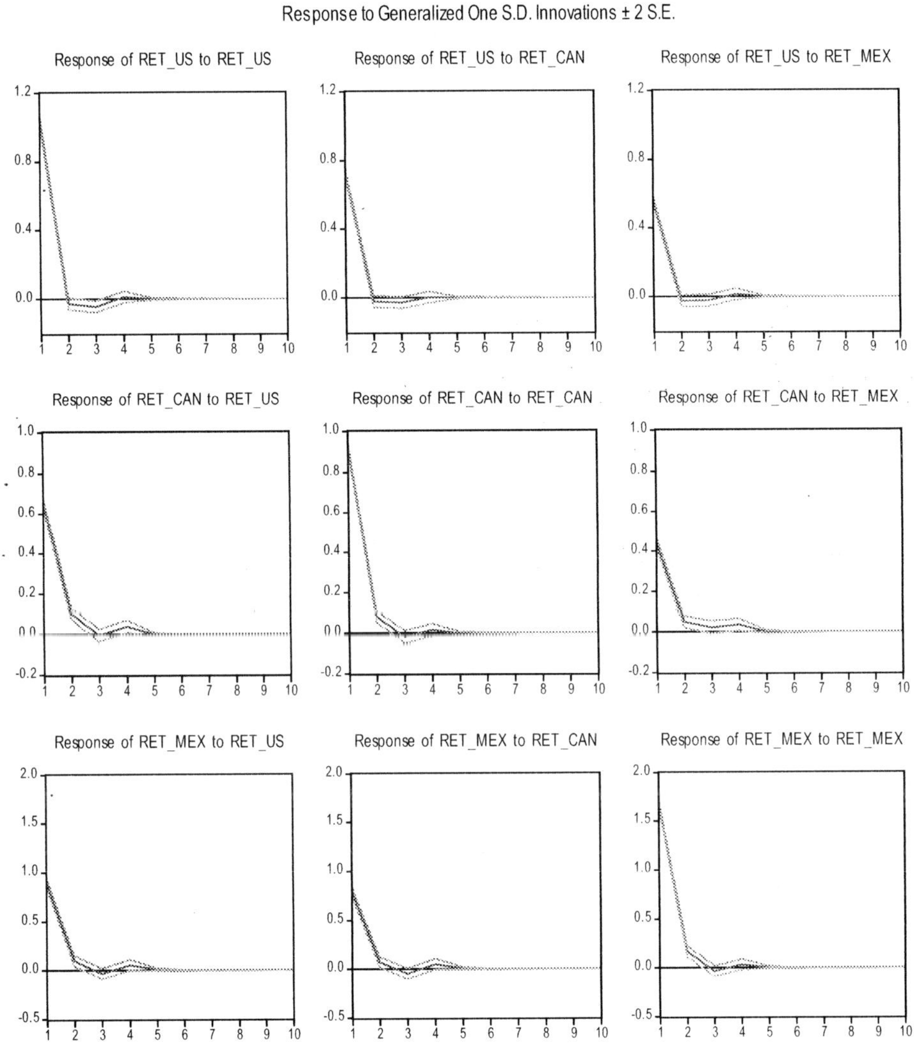

Figure 5.1. Generalized Impulse-response Functions to 1 SD in Stock Market Returns.

Table 5.1. Generalized Impulse Response of US Returns

	One Standard Deviation in		
Period	**US Market**	**Canadian Market**	**Mexican Market**
1	1.034037	0.723898	0.553128
	(0.01169)	(0.01389)	(0.01522)
2	-0.027797	-0.021308	-0.024413
	(0.01682)	(0.01684)	(0.01686)
3	-0.044758	-0.028887	-0.021987
	(0.01663)	(0.01679)	(0.01673)
4	0.010966	0.001436	0.013743
	(0.01622)	(0.01670)	(0.01632)
5	6.11E-05	-0.000301	0.000643
	(0.00391)	(0.00288)	(0.00309)
6	-0.000984	-0.000333	-0.001335
	(0.00194)	(0.00162)	(0.00183)
7	-4.55E-05	0.000171	-0.000165
	(0.00103)	(0.00084)	(0.00091)
8	0.000106	9.72E-05	7.90E-05
	(0.00025)	(0.00022)	(0.00021)
9	5.37E-06	-1.57E-05	1.91E-05
	(0.00015)	(0.00012)	(0.00014)
10	2.06E-06	-6.03E-06	6.58E-06
	(4.8E-05)	(4.1E-05)	(4.4E-05)

Note: Period equals the number of days since the innovation. Numbers in parentheses equal standard errors calculated through a Monte Carlo simulation with 1,000 repetitions.

Second, stock returns respond immediately to a shock in other markets, implying that the markets process information quickly, but do not show long-lasting effects. In all cases, the response dies out within two days.

Third, the response of each market to shocks in its own market always exceeds the response to shocks in other markets. For example, the response of US returns to shocks in the US market prove more than double the response of US returns to shocks originating in the Mexican market. The response of Mexican returns to shocks in the US market equals about half the response of the Mexican returns to shocks originating in its own market.

Table 5.2. Generalized Impulse Response of Canadian Returns

	One Standard Deviation in		
Period	**US Market**	**Canadian Market**	**Mexican Market**
1	0.642031	0.917095	0.435253
	(0.01235)	(0.01048)	(0.01421)
2	0.100003	0.079624	0.048547
	(0.01514)	(0.01504)	(0.01492)
3	-0.005393	-0.019550	0.021343
	(0.01524)	(0.01529)	(0.01521)
4	0.037463	0.014930	0.034610
	(0.01531)	(0.01561)	(0.01480)
5	-0.002220	-0.002699	-0.000688
	(0.00371)	(0.00385)	(0.00388)
6	-0.002773	-0.000985	-0.002715
	(0.00189)	(0.00151)	(0.00179)
7	0.000259	0.000476	1.78E-05
	(0.00113)	(0.00106)	(0.00114)
8	0.000151	0.000141	0.000119
	(0.00032)	(0.00028)	(0.00025)
9	1.43E-05	-1.97E-05	2.65E-05
	(0.00016)	(0.00013)	(0.00014)
10	8.02E-06	-5.95E-06	1.38E-05
	(5.8E-05)	(5.4E-05)	(5.7E-05)

Note: See Table 5.1.

Fourth, a shock to returns in Canada produce a larger response in Mexico and the US than a shock to returns in Mexico and the US produce on the returns in Canada. Similarly, a shock to the returns in the US produce a larger response in Mexico than a shock on returns in Mexico produces on returns in the US.

Finally, the US holds the leading role, in the sense that the Canadian (Mexican) market responds more to shocks stemming from the US than from Mexico (Canada). Nonetheless, the US market also responds to shocks originating in Mexico and Canada. Hence, the US market leads, but is not autonomous.

Table 5.3. Generalized Impulse Response of Mexican Returns

	One Standard Deviation in		
Period	**US market**	**Canadian market**	**Mexican market**
1	0.890224	0.789836	1.664216
	(0.02518)	(0.02619)	(0.01954)
2	0.095020	0.070445	0.166250
	(0.02691)	(0.02647)	(0.02670)
3	-0.034335	-0.049562	-0.034957
	(0.02695)	(0.02663)	(0.02777)
4	0.053834	0.048747	0.031622
	(0.02672)	(0.02657)	(0.02629)
5	0.007165	0.007756	0.003003
	(0.00621)	(0.00643)	(0.00684)
6	-0.004174	-0.002791	-0.002314
	(0.00327)	(0.00248)	(0.00305)
7	0.001318	0.000381	0.001458
	(0.00194)	(0.00162)	(0.00182)
8	0.000299	7.14E-05	0.000325
	(0.00050)	(0.00051)	(0.00051)
9	-0.000146	-7.58E-05	-0.000141
	(0.00025)	(0.00020)	(0.00024)
10	-1.66E-05	7.22E-06	-2.65E-05
	(9.5E-05)	(8.6E-05)	(0.00010)

Note: See Table 5.1.

Chapter 6

The Multivariate GARCH: Method and Econometrics

Shocks affect not only returns, but also volatilities. The ARCH model originally developed by Engle (1982) and generalized by Bollerslev (1986) provides the most popular method for modelling volatility of stock market returns. In recent years, many studies, starting with Bollerslev, Engle, and Wooldridge (1988), extend the univariate GARCH model of Bollerslev (1986) to the multivariate case for modelling the volatility of multiple asset returns.[1]

6.1. Issues and Stylized Facts

Multivariate GARCH models provide several advantages over univariate GARCH models (Bauwens et al., 2006). First, they explicitly accommodate inter-market dependencies in the conditional mean and/or conditional variance equations, thereby avoiding multi-step estimation procedures for univariate models. Second, they improve the efficiency and the power of the tests for cross-market co-movements and spillovers. Third, they produce meaningful analysis of many issues in asset pricing and portfolio allocation that require a multivariate context (Bollerslev et al., 1992). Finally, they accommodate covariances that

---

[1] One can model the interdependence across markets using both univariate and multivariate GARCH models. Papers that employ univariate GARCH models include Hamao et al. (1990) and Hahm (2004), who model the volatility spillovers across stock markets; Jiang and Chiang (2000) and Fang (2001), who model the volatility spillovers across stock and foreign exchange markets; and Najand and Yung (1997), who model the price dynamics in exchange rates, stock index, and Treasury bonds in futures markets.

capture the inter-relatedness of economic variables and their behavior in reacting to the same information (Bera and Higgins, 1993).

Two problems exist in extending the univariate GARCH models to a multivariate framework (Bauwens et al., 2006). First, the number of parameters to estimate grows rapidly with the dimension of the model, the "curse of dimensionality." Second, finding a specification that maintains the positive definiteness of the covariance matrix may prove difficult. Recent contributions to the multivariate GARCH literature confront these difficulties by imposing a variety of simplifying restrictions (Bauwens et al., 2006).

Several important stylized facts emerge from empirical research on asset returns. First, researchers typically observe asymmetry in volatilities and covariances. Asymmetric volatility, a well know phenomenon, receives much discussion in the literature, especially the asymmetric effects of shocks on the second moment of stock returns in univariate GARCH models. Black (1976) and Christie (1982) propose the "leverage-effect" explanation for such asymmetry in variance. As equity values fall, the weight attached to debt in a firm's capital structure rises, *ceteris paribus*. This induces equity holders, who bear the residual risk of the firm, to perceive the stream of future income accruing to their portfolios comes with relatively more risk. Campbell and Hentschel (1992) and Poterba and Summers (1986) provide the alternative "volatility-feedback"' hypothesis. Assuming constant dividends, stock prices should fall when volatility rises, when expected returns increase with stock return volatility.[2]

Second, researchers also typically observe skewness and kurtosis in asset returns. Financial returns rarely follow normal distributions. The estimation of multivariate GARCH models commonly maximizes a Gaussian likelihood function. We can justify the normality assumption because the Gaussian quasi-ML estimator proves inefficient, but consistent, provided we specify the conditional mean and the conditional variance correctly (Bollerslev and Wooldridge, 1992). Various techniques exist to deal with the questionable normality assumption. Harvey et al. (1994), Fiorentini et al. (2003), and Kan and Zhou (2006) replace the multivariate Gaussian density with the Student density, which incorporates fat tails.[3] Since the *t*-distribution adds only one more

[2] Pagan and Schwert (1990), Nelson (1991), Campbell and Hentschel (1992), Engle and Ng (1993), Glosten et al. (1993), and Henry (1998), among others, report evidence of asymmetry in equity-return volatility using univariate GARCH models. Kroner and Ng (1998), Braun et al. (1995), Henry and Sharma (1999), Engle and Cho (1999) and Brooks and Henry (2000), Ang and Chen (2002), Kearney and Poti (2006) among others, use multivariate GARCH models to capture time variation and asymmetry in the variance–covariance structure of asset returns.

[3] Several other alternative distributions appear in empirical research, including the mixture of multivariate normal densities (Vlaar and Palm, 1993; Haas et al., 2006), the generalized

parameter, this parsimonious extension, which nests the normal as a special case, captures the observed fat tails or leptokurtic characteristics of financial data. Furthermore, although symmetric, the *t*-distribution's highly volatile sample skewness can generate the skewness of the data with high probability. Kan and Zhou (2006) note that the finite sample variation of the sample skewness of a *t*-distribution proves very large for small degrees of freedom. Thus, a high probability for observing large sample skewness occurs even though the true distribution is symmetric.

6.2. Econometric Framework

The econometric model that we use to investigate returns and volatility dynamics between the three North-American stock markets includes two parts – the mean and covariance models.

The Mean Model

Equation (6.1) models the North-American index returns as a VAR(3) process:

$$R_t = \mu + \sum_{i=1}^{3} \Gamma_i R_{t-i} + \varepsilon_t \,.^{4} \tag{6.1}$$

We can write equation (6.1) in extended form as follows:

$$\begin{bmatrix} r_t^{US} \\ r_t^{MEX} \\ r_t^{CAN} \end{bmatrix} = \begin{bmatrix} \mu^{US} \\ \mu^{MEX} \\ \mu^{CAN} \end{bmatrix} + \begin{bmatrix} \gamma_{11}^1 & \gamma_{12}^1 & \gamma_{13}^1 \\ \gamma_{21}^1 & \gamma_{22}^1 & \gamma_{23}^1 \\ \gamma_{31}^1 & \gamma_{32}^1 & \gamma_{33}^1 \end{bmatrix} \begin{bmatrix} r_{t-1}^{US} \\ r_{t-1}^{MEX} \\ r_{t-1}^{CAN} \end{bmatrix} + \begin{bmatrix} \gamma_{11}^2 & \gamma_{12}^2 & \gamma_{13}^2 \\ \gamma_{21}^2 & \gamma_{22}^2 & \gamma_{23}^2 \\ \gamma_{31}^2 & \gamma_{32}^2 & \gamma_{33}^2 \end{bmatrix} \begin{bmatrix} r_{t-2}^{US} \\ r_{t-2}^{MEX} \\ r_{t-2}^{CAN} \end{bmatrix}$$

hyperbolic distribution (Barndorff-Nielsen and Shepard, 2004; Mencía and Sentana, 2004), the multivariate skew-Student density (Bauwens and Laurent, 2005), and the asymmetric multivariate Laplace (Kozubowski and Podgorski, 2001; Cajigas and Urga, 2006). Bollerslev and Wooldridge (1992) note, however, that if the researcher chooses an incorrect non-normal distribution, then the parameter estimates of the multivariate GARCH are not even consistent.

[4] Note that we do not incorporate the error correction terms into the mean equations, because we do not reject the null hypothesis of no cointegration.

$$+\begin{bmatrix} \gamma_{11}^3 & \gamma_{12}^3 & \gamma_{13}^3 \\ \gamma_{21}^3 & \gamma_{22}^3 & \gamma_{23}^3 \\ \gamma_{31}^3 & \gamma_{32}^3 & \gamma_{33}^3 \end{bmatrix} \begin{bmatrix} r_{t-3}^{US} \\ r_{t-3}^{MEX} \\ r_{t-3}^{CAN} \end{bmatrix} + \begin{bmatrix} \varepsilon_t^{US} \\ \varepsilon_t^{MEX} \\ \varepsilon_t^{CAN} \end{bmatrix}, \quad (6.2)$$

where R_t equals a (3 x 1) vector of daily returns, with r_t^{US}, r_t^{MEX} and r_t^{CAN}, representing the returns from S&P 500, IPC, and S&P/TSX indices, respectively; μ equals a (3 x 1) vector of constants; Γ_i i = 1, 2, 3 equal (3 x 3) matrices of parameters; and ε_t equals a (3 x 1) vector of innovations or "news."

The multivariate structure of equations (60) or (61) provides measures of the significance of the own and cross-mean spillovers. The off-diagonal elements, $\gamma_{i,j}^1$, $\gamma_{i,j}^2$, and $\gamma_{i,j}^3$ for i = 1, 2, 3 capture the effects of interactions in means, also known as return spillover. The diagonal elements, $\gamma_{i,i}^1$, $\gamma_{i,i}^2$, and $\gamma_{i,i}^3$ for i = 1, 2, 3 measure the effects of own past returns. If the off-diagonal elements equal zero, then the model excludes the return transmission across the markets, which we can test using Wald statistics.

The Covariance Model

In the GARCH framework, the conditional distribution of ε_t varies with time with the following specification:

$$e_t | \Omega_{t-1} \sim D(0, H_t) \quad (6.3)$$

where H_t equals a (3 x 3) time-varying conditional covariance matrix.

Several well known multivariate GARCH specifications include the VECH model of Bollerslev et al. (1988), the CCC model of Bollerslev (1990), the DCC model of Engle (2002), the BEKK model of Engle and Kroner (1995), the Asymmetric BEKK model of Kroner and Ng (1998), the Vector Autoregressive Moving Average GARCH (VARMA-GARCH) model of Ling and McAleer (2003), the VARMA Asymmetric GARCH (VARMA-AGARCH) model of McAleer et al. (2008), and the multivariate EGARCH of Koutmos and Booth

(1995). Each model offers certain advantages and disadvantages, and each model imposes different restrictions and specifications on the conditional covariance.

We model the variance-covariance matrix $H_t = \left[h_{ij,t} \right]$ as an asymmetric BEKK-GARCH(1,1) model (Kroner and Ng, 1998). The BEKK specification ensures a positive-definite H_t by imposing quadratic forms on the matrices of coefficients. This sufficiently general specification allows the conditional variances and covariances to interact with each other and although computationally complex, does not require the estimation of a large number of parameters. We can write the asymmetric BEKK parameterization as follows:

$$H_t = C'C + A'\varepsilon_{t-1}\varepsilon'_{t-1}A + B'H_{t-1}B + G'\eta_{t-1}\eta'_{t-1}G, \qquad (6.4)$$

where *C*, *A*, *B*, and *G* equal (3 *x* 3) matrices of parameters with a lower-triangular *C*; H_t equals the (3 *x* 3) conditional covariance; $\varepsilon_t = [\varepsilon_{1t}, \varepsilon_{2t}, \varepsilon_{3t}]$ equals a vector of unexpected shocks from the VAR(3) model; and $\eta_t = [\eta_{1t}, \eta_{2t}, \eta_{3t}]$ equals a vector that contain the Glosten et al. (1993) series defined as η_{it} = min[ε_{it}, 0], where η_{it} equals ε_{it}, if ε_{it} when negative and zero otherwise, and h_{ijt} equals the conditional second moment series. In expanded form, we can write the asymmetric BEKK GARCH (1,1) model as follows:

$$H_t = \begin{bmatrix} c_{11} & 0 & 0 \\ c_{21} & c_{22} & 0 \\ c_{31} & c_{32} & c_{33} \end{bmatrix}' \begin{bmatrix} c_{11} & 0 & 0 \\ c_{21} & c_{22} & 0 \\ c_{31} & c_{32} & c_{33} \end{bmatrix}$$

$$+ \begin{bmatrix} a_{11} & a_{12} & a_{13} \\ a_{21} & a_{22} & a_{23} \\ a_{31} & a_{32} & a_{33} \end{bmatrix}' \begin{bmatrix} \varepsilon^2_{1,t-1} & \varepsilon_{1,t-1}\varepsilon_{2,t-1} & \varepsilon_{1,t-1}\varepsilon_{3,t-1} \\ \varepsilon_{2,t-1}\varepsilon_{1,t-1} & \varepsilon^2_{2,t-1} & \varepsilon_{2,t-1}\varepsilon_{3,t-1} \\ \varepsilon_{3,t-1}\varepsilon_{1,t-1} & \varepsilon_{3,t-1}\varepsilon_{2,t-1} & \varepsilon^2_{3,t-1} \end{bmatrix} \begin{bmatrix} a_{11} & a_{12} & a_{13} \\ a_{21} & a_{22} & a_{23} \\ a_{31} & a_{32} & a_{33} \end{bmatrix}$$

$$+ \begin{bmatrix} b_{11} & b_{12} & b_{13} \\ b_{21} & b_{22} & b_{23} \\ b_{31} & b_{32} & b_{33} \end{bmatrix}' \begin{bmatrix} h_{11,t-1} & h_{12,t-1} & h_{13,t-1} \\ h_{21,t-1} & h_{22,t-1} & h_{23,t-1} \\ h_{31,t-1} & h_{32,t-1} & h_{33,t-1} \end{bmatrix} \begin{bmatrix} b_{11} & b_{12} & b_{13} \\ b_{21} & b_{22} & b_{23} \\ b_{31} & b_{32} & b_{33} \end{bmatrix}$$

$$+\begin{bmatrix} g_{11} & g_{12} & g_{13} \\ g_{21} & g_{22} & g_{23} \\ g_{31} & g_{32} & g_{33} \end{bmatrix}' \begin{bmatrix} \eta_{1,t-1}^2 & \eta_{1,t-1}\eta_{2,t-1} & \eta_{1,t-1}\eta_{3,t-1} \\ \eta_{2,t-1}\eta_{1,t-1} & \eta_{2,t-1}^2 & \eta_{2,t-1}\eta_{3,t-1} \\ \eta_{3,t-1}\eta_{1,t-1} & \eta_{3,t-1}\eta_{2,t-1} & \eta_{3,t-1}^2 \end{bmatrix} \begin{bmatrix} g_{11} & g_{12} & g_{13} \\ g_{21} & g_{22} & g_{23} \\ g_{31} & g_{32} & g_{33} \end{bmatrix} \quad (6.5)$$

The symmetric specification restricts $g_{ij} = 0$ for all $i, j = 1, 2, 3$, and $i \neq j$. Kroner and Ng (1998) analyze the asymmetric properties of time-varying covariance matrix models, identifying three possible forms of asymmetric behavior.[5] First, the covariance matrix displays owń- variance asymmetry, if the sign of the innovation in $r_{i,t}$ affects the conditional variance of $r_{i,t}$. Second, the covariance matrix exhibits cross-variance asymmetry, if the sign of the innovation in $r_{j,t}$, for $i \neq j$, affects the conditional variance of $r_{i,t}$. Third, if the sign of the innovation in $r_{i,t}$ affects the conditional covariance of $r_{i,t}$ and $r_{j,t}$, the model displays own covariance asymmetry. See discussion following equations (65a), (65b), and (65c) for more details. Finally, if the sign of the innovations in $r_{i,t}$ affects the conditional covariance of $r_{j,t}$ and $r_{k,t}$, $i \neq j$ *or* k, then the model displays cross-covariance asymmetry. See discussion following equations (66a), (66b), and (66c) for more details.

We can expand equation (6.5) by matrix multiplication. The ith conditional variance, $h_{ii,t}$, $i = 1, 2, 3$, equals the following:

To illustrate own-variance asymmetry, consider equation (6.6a). If g_{11} is significant, then asymmetry enters the conditional variance, $h_{11,t}$, through $\varepsilon_{1,t-1}^2 = \eta_{1,t-1}^2$, when $\varepsilon_{1,t} < 0$. Similarly, to illustrate cross-covariance asymmetry, consider equation (6.6a). If g_{21} is significant, then an asymmetry enters the conditional variance, $h_{11,t}$, through $\varepsilon_{2,t-1}^2 = \eta_{2,t-1}^2$, when $\varepsilon_{2,t} < 0$. We illustrate

[5] As a preliminary test, we apply the Engle and Ng (1993) test for asymmetry in volatility to each of the three return series. We find that each returns series exhibits negative sign and size bias, suggesting asymmetry and "bad news" matters more than "good news." The t-ratios for the negative sign bias equal 4.2606 (US), 3.1024 (Mexico), and 3.6336 (Canada). The t-ratios for the negative size bias equal -12.0266 (US), -11.7938 (Mexico), and -8.5936 (Canada). The chi-square values of the joint test (df = 3) computed as TR2 equal 698.579 (US), 610.907 (Mexico) and 480.553 (Canada).

the two covariance asymmetry results following equations (6.7a), (6.7b), and (6.7c).

$$
\begin{aligned}
h_{11,t} = {} & c_{11}^2 + a_{11}^2\varepsilon_{1,t-1}^2 + a_{21}^2\varepsilon_{2,t-1}^2 + a_{31}^2\varepsilon_{3,t-1}^2 + 2a_{11}a_{21}\varepsilon_{1,t-1}\varepsilon_{2,t-1} \\
& + 2a_{11}a_{31}\varepsilon_{1,t-1}\varepsilon_{3,t-1} + 2a_{21}a_{31}\varepsilon_{2,t-1}\varepsilon_{3,t-1} + b_{11}^2h_{11,t-1} + b_{21}^2h_{22,t-1} \\
& + b_{31}^2h_{33,t-1} + 2b_{11}b_{21}h_{12,t-1} + 2b_{11}b_{31}h_{13,t-1} + 2b_{21}b_{31}h_{23,t-1} + g_{11}^2\eta_{1,t-1}^2 \\
& + g_{21}^2\eta_{2,t-1}^2 + g_{31}^2\eta_{3,t-1}^2 + 2g_{11}g_{21}\eta_{1,t-1}\eta_{2,t-1} + 2g_{11}g_{31}\eta_{1,t-1}\eta_{3,t-1} \\
& + 2g_{21}g_{31}\eta_{2,t-1}\eta_{3,t-1}
\end{aligned}
\tag{6.6a}
$$

$$
\begin{aligned}
h_{22,t} = {} & c_{12}^2 + c_{22}^2 + a_{12}^2\varepsilon_{1,t-1}^2 + a_{22}^2\varepsilon_{2,t-1}^2 + a_{32}^2\varepsilon_{3,t-1}^2 + 2a_{12}a_{22}\varepsilon_{1,t-1}\varepsilon_{2,t-1} \\
& + 2a_{12}a_{32}\varepsilon_{1,t-1}\varepsilon_{3,t-1} + 2a_{22}a_{32}\varepsilon_{2,t-1}\varepsilon_{3,t-1} + b_{12}^2h_{11,t-1} + b_{22}^2h_{22,t-1} \\
& + b_{32}^2h_{33,t-1} + 2b_{12}b_{22}h_{12,t-1} + 2b_{12}b_{32}h_{13,t-1} + 2b_{22}b_{32}h_{23,t-1} + g_{12}^2\eta_{1,t-1}^2 \\
& + g_{22}^2\eta_{2,t-1}^2 + g_{32}^2\eta_{3,t-1}^2 + 2g_{12}g_{22}\eta_{1,t-1}\eta_{2,t-1} + 2g_{12}g_{32}\eta_{1,t-1}\eta_{3,t-1} \\
& + 2g_{22}g_{32}\eta_{2,t-1}\eta_{3,t-1}
\end{aligned}
\tag{6.6b}
$$

$$
\begin{aligned}
h_{33,t} = {} & c_{13}^2 + c_{23}^2 + c_{33}^2 + a_{13}^2\varepsilon_{1,t-1}^2 + a_{23}^2\varepsilon_{2,t-1}^2 + a_{33}^2\varepsilon_{3,t-1}^2 + 2a_{13}a_{23}\varepsilon_{1,t-1}\varepsilon_{2,t-1} \\
& + 2a_{13}a_{33}\varepsilon_{1,t-1}\varepsilon_{3,t-1} + 2a_{23}a_{33}\varepsilon_{2,t-1}\varepsilon_{3,t-1} + b_{13}^2h_{11,t-1} + b_{23,t-1}^2h_{22,t-1} \\
& + b_{33}^2h_{33,t-1} + 2b_{13}b_{23}h_{12,t-1} + 2b_{13}b_{33}h_{13,t-1} + 2b_{23}b_{33}h_{23,t-1} + g_{13}^2\eta_{1,t-1}^2 \\
& + g_{23}^2\eta_{2,t-1}^2 + g_{33}^2\eta_{3,t-1}^2 + 2g_{13}g_{23}\eta_{1,t-1}\eta_{2,t-1} + 2g_{13}g_{33}\eta_{1,t-1}\eta_{3,t-1} \\
& + 2g_{23}g_{33}\eta_{2,t-1}\eta_{3,t-1}
\end{aligned}
\tag{6.6c}
$$

Similarly, we can write the ith, j^{th} conditional covariance, $h_{ij,t}$, $i \neq j,\ i,j = 1,\ 2,\ 3$ as follows:

$$\begin{aligned} h_{12,t} = h_{21,t} &= c_{11}c_{12} + a_{12}a_{11}\varepsilon^2_{1,t-1} + a_{22}a_{21}\varepsilon^2_{2,t-1} + a_{32}a_{31}\varepsilon^2_{3,t-1} \\ &+ (a_{12}a_{21} + a_{11}a_{22})\varepsilon_{1,t-1}\varepsilon_{2,t-1} + (a_{12}a_{31} + a_{32}a_{11})\varepsilon_{1,t-1}\varepsilon_{3,t-1} \\ &+ (a_{22}a_{31} + a_{32}a_{21})\varepsilon_{2,t-1}\varepsilon_{3,t-1} + b_{12}b_{11}h_{11,t-1} + b_{22}b_{21}h_{22,t-1} \\ &+ b_{32}b_{31}h_{33,t-1} + b_{22}b_{11}h_{12,t-1} + b_{32}b_{11}h_{13,t-1} + b_{12}b_{21}h_{21,t-1} \\ &+ b_{12}b_{31}h_{31,t-1} + b_{32}b_{21}h_{23,t-1} + b_{22}b_{31}h_{32,t-1} + g_{12}g_{11}\eta^2_{1,t-1} \\ &+ g_{22}g_{21}\eta^2_{2,t-1} + g_{32}g_{31}\eta^2_{3,t-1} + (g_{12}g_{21} + g_{11}g_{22})\eta_{1,t-1}\eta_{2,t-1} \\ &+ (g_{12}g_{31} + g_{32}g_{11})\eta_{1,t-1}\eta_{3,t-1} + (g_{22}g_{31} + g_{32}g_{21})\eta_{2,t-1}\eta_{3,t-1} \end{aligned} \tag{6.7a}$$

$$\begin{aligned} h_{13,t} = h_{31,t} &= c_{11}c_{13} + a_{13}a_{11}\varepsilon^2_{1,t-1} + a_{23}a_{21}\varepsilon^2_{2,t-1} + a_{33}a_{31}\varepsilon^2_{3,t-1} \\ &+ (a_{13}a_{21} + a_{23}a_{11})\varepsilon_{1,t-1}\varepsilon_{2,t-1} + (a_{13}a_{31} + a_{33}a_{11})\varepsilon_{1,t-1}\varepsilon_{3,t-1} \\ &+ (a_{23}a_{31} + a_{33}a_{21})\varepsilon_{2,t-1}\varepsilon_{3,t-1} + b_{13}b_{11}h_{11,t-1} + b_{23}b_{21}h_{22,t-1} \\ &+ b_{33}b_{31}h_{33,t-1} + b_{23}b_{11}h_{12,t-1} + b_{33}b_{11}h_{13,t-1} + b_{13}b_{21}h_{21,t-1} \\ &+ b_{13}b_{31}h_{31,t-1} + b_{33}b_{21}h_{23,t-1} + b_{23}b_{31}h_{32,t-1} + g_{13}a_{11}\eta^2_{1,t-1} \\ &+ g_{23}g_{21}\eta^2_{2,t-1} + g_{33}g_{31}\eta^2_{3,t-1} + (g_{13}g_{21} + g_{23}g_{11})\eta_{1,t-1}\eta_{2,t-1} \\ &+ (g_{13}g_{31} + g_{33}g_{11})\eta_{1,t-1}\eta_{3,t-1} + (g_{23}g_{31} + g_{33}g_{21})\eta_{2,t-1}\eta_{3,t-1} \end{aligned} \tag{6.7b}$$

$$\begin{aligned} h_{23,t} = h_{32,t} &= c_{12}c_{13} + c_{22}c_{23} + a_{13}a_{12}\varepsilon^2_{1,t-1} + a_{23}a_{22}\varepsilon^2_{2,t-1} + a_{32}a_{33}\varepsilon^2_{3,t-1} \\ &+ (a_{12}a_{23} + a_{13}a_{22})\varepsilon_{1,t-1}\varepsilon_{2,t-1} + (a_{13}a_{32} + a_{33}a_{12})\varepsilon_{1,t-1}\varepsilon_{3,t-1} \\ &+ (a_{23}a_{32} + a_{33}a_{22})\varepsilon_{2,t-1}\varepsilon_{3,t-1} + b_{12}b_{12}h_{11,t-1} + b_{23}b_{22}h_{22,t-1} \\ &+ b_{32}b_{33}h_{33,t-1} + b_{23}b_{12}h_{12,t-1} + b_{33}b_{12}h_{13,t-1} + b_{13}b_{22}h_{21,t-1} \\ &+ b_{33}b_{21}h_{31,t-1} + b_{33}b_{22}h_{23,t-1} + b_{23}b_{32}h_{32,t-1} + g_{13}g_{12}\eta^2_{1,t-1} \\ &+ g_{23}g_{22}\eta^2_{2,t-1} + g_{32}g_{33}\eta^2_{3,t-1} + (g_{12}g_{23} + g_{13}g_{22})\eta_{1,t-1}\eta_{2,t-1} \\ &+ (g_{13}g_{32} + g_{33}g_{12})\eta_{1,t-1}\eta_{3,t-1} + (g_{23}g_{32} + g_{33}g_{22})\eta_{2,t-1}\eta_{3,t-1} \end{aligned} \tag{6.7c}$$

To illustrate own-covariance asymmetry, consider equation (6.7a). If g_{12} and g_{11} are significant, then an asymmetry enters the conditional covariance,

$h_{12,t} = h_{21,t}$, through $\varepsilon_{1,t-1}^2 = \eta_{1,t-1}^2$, when $\varepsilon_{1,t} < 0$. Similarly, to illustrate cross-covariance asymmetry, consider equation (6.7a). If g_{32} and g_{11} are significant, then an asymmetry enters the conditional covariance, $h_{12,t} = h_{21,t}$, through $\varepsilon_{3,t-1}^2 = \eta_{3,t-1}^2$, when $\varepsilon_{3,t} < 0$.

We estimate the VAR(3)-BEKK-GARCH(1,1) model by non-linear ML method. This requires the specification of the distribution for the 3-dimentional innovations. We assume two distributional forms for the innovations. First, the most common and convenient distribution is the multivariate normal. In this case, the log-likelihood function equals the following:

$$L(\theta) = -\frac{T}{2} K \ln(2\pi) - \frac{1}{2}\sum_{t=1}^{T}(\ln|H_t| + \hat{\varepsilon}_t' H_t^{-1} \hat{\varepsilon}_t), \tag{6.8}$$

where T represents the number of observations, K equals the number of variables, and θ represents the vector of unknown parameters in the conditional means, and the C, A, B, and G matrices describe the conditional variance.

Second, we use the multivariate Student-t density, which accommodates leptokurtic data. Compared to the multivariate normal distribution, the multivariate Student-t distribution does not impose a computational burden and only adds one additional parameter, the degrees of freedom (υ), in the calculation of the log-likelihood function. That is,

$$\begin{aligned} L(\theta) = \sum_{i=1}^{T}\left[ln\Gamma\left(\frac{\upsilon+K}{2}\right) - ln\Gamma\left(\frac{\upsilon}{2}\right) - \frac{K}{2} ln(\upsilon-2)\pi \right] \\ -\frac{1}{2}\sum_{i=1}^{T}\left[ln|H_t| + (\upsilon+K) ln\left(1 + \frac{\hat{\varepsilon}_t' H_t^{-1}\hat{\varepsilon}_t}{\upsilon-2}\right)\right], \end{aligned} \tag{6.9}$$

where Γ is the (complete) gamma function and υ equals the degrees of freedom. The mth moment of the multivariate Student-t distribution exists, if $\upsilon > m$. Consequently, we impose the restriction that $\upsilon > 2$. As υ approaches infinity, the multivariate Student-t distribution approaches the multivariate normal distribution. Although symmetric, the multivariate Student-t distribution exhibits fatter tails than the multivariate normal distribution. The coefficient of excess (relative to the normal) kurtosis is given by $\kappa = 2/(\upsilon - 4)$.

Chapter 7

THE MULTIVARIATE GARCH: ESTIMATION RESULTS

This Chapter reports the results of our estimations. Table 7.1 reports the parameter estimates for the standard (symmetric) BEKK specification and the asymmetric BEKK specification, using both distributional assumptions – normal and Student-*t* distributions. We estimate the models for the first moment simultaneously with those for the second moment using the BFGS (Broyden, 1970; Fletcher, 1970; Goldfarb, 1970; Shanno, 1970) algorithm. In what follows, US = 1, Mexico = 2, and Canada = 3.

Table 7.1. Estimates of VAR(3)-BEKK-GARCH(1,1) 1992-2007

Panel 1. The VAR(3) Model : The Mean Equations

Variable	Normal Distribution		*t*-Distribution	
	Symmetric	Asymmetric	Symmetric	Asymmetric
		US Stock Market		
constant	0.0612	0.0391	0.0658	0.0517
	(3.3963)	(4.4454)	(5.6895)	(5.3687)
r_{t-1}^{US}	-0.0224	-0.0173	-0.0391	-0.0311
	(1.2379)	(2.0634)	(2.4541)	(2.5083)
r_{t-2}^{US}	-0.0299	-0.0275	-0.0360	-0.0369
	(1.6643)	(2.1814)	(2.2056)	(3.5259)

Table 7.1. Continued

Variable	Normal Distribution		t-Distribution	
	Symmetric	Asymmetric	Symmetric	Asymmetric
		US Stock Market		
r_{t-3}^{US}	-0.0034	-0.0016	-0.0207	0.0123
	(0.1839)	(0.2185)	(1.3882)	(1.0758)
r_{t-1}^{MEX}	0.0046	0.0051	0.0080	0.0057
	(0.5633)	(0.9635)	(1.0256)	(0.9703)
r_{t-2}^{MEX}	-0.0028	-0.0003	0.0007	0.0021
	(0.3658)	(0.0495)	(0.0959)	(0.3275)
r_{t-3}^{MEX}	0.0078	0.0115	0.0021	0.0047
	(0.7731)	(2.0971)	(0.2701)	(0.7642)
r_{t-1}^{CAN}	0.0296	0.0228	0.0335	0.0275
	(1.3647)	(2.7614)	(2.0084)	(2.0917)
r_{t-2}^{CAN}	-0.0013	-0.0014	-0.0280	-0.0221
	(0.0597)	(0.1120)	(1.5459)	(1.8252)
r_{t-3}^{CAN}	-0.0136	-0.0153	0.0027	-0.0045
	(0.6044)	(1.6424)	(0.1656)	(0.3646)
		Mexican Stock Market		
constant	0.1305	0.0877	0.1272	0.0989
	(4.6172)	(4.6300)	(6.4951)	(6.1046)
r_{t-1}^{MEX}	0.1097	0.1169	0.1135	0.1143
	(4.8006)	(10.2507)	(6.9250)	(10.1196)
r_{t-2}^{MEX}	-0.0359	-0.0204	-0.0357	-0.0262
	(1.7162)	(1.6493)	(2.2639)	(2.1753)
r_{t-3}^{MEX}	-0.0033	0.0089	-0.0102	-0.0029
	(0.1571)	(0.6836)	(0.6476)	(0.2477)
r_{t-1}^{US}	0.0111	0.0096	0.0085	0.0126
	(0.3118)	(0.6512)	(0.3264)	(0.6944)
r_{t-2}^{US}	0.0048	0.0000	-0.0036	-0.0061
	(0.1449)	(0.0011)	(0.1316)	(0.3550)
r_{t-3}^{US}	0.0470	0.0395	0.0222	0.0284
	(1.1517)	(2.2688)	(0.8486)	(1.6042)
r_{t-1}^{CAN}	0.0547	0.0534	0.0384	0.0385
	(1.3322)	(3.8479)	(1.3288)	(1.8086)

Table 7.1. Continued

Variable	Normal Distribution		t-Distribution	
	Symmetric	Asymmetric	Symmetric	Asymmetric
		US Stock Market		
r_{t-2}^{CAN}	0.0017	-0.0191	-0.0377	-0.0385
	(0.0443)	(1.0601)	(1.2125)	(1.7519)
r_{t-3}^{CAN}	0.0137	0.0174	0.0246	0.0216
	(0.3015)	(0.9612)	(0.8149)	(1.0732)
		Canadian Stock Market		
constant	0.0554	0.0411	0.0644	0.0559
	(3.4761)	(4.0530)	(6.2808)	(6.5967)
r_{t-1}^{CAN}	0.0594	0.0638	0.0520	0.0552
	(3.0157)	(6.0731)	(3.2990)	(4.4573)
r_{t-2}^{CAN}	-0.0327	-0.0278	-0.0448	-0.0414
	(1.8861)	(2.3505)	(2.7502)	(3.8917)
r_{t-3}^{CAN}	-0.0364	-0.0325	-0.0223	-0.0243
	(1.9121)	(3.4403)	(1.4836)	(2.1751)
r_{t-1}^{US}	0.0722	0.0749	0.0709	0.0734
	(4.4425)	(9.2269)	(5.1388)	(6.9300)
r_{t-2}^{US}	0.0109	0.0105	-0.0003	0.0009
	(0.5772)	(0.9985)	(0.0210)	(0.0911)
r_{t-3}^{US}	0.0513	0.0459	0.0339	0.0359
	(2.8510)	(5.8329)	(2.5637)	(3.7102)
r_{t-1}^{MEX}	0.0114	0.0113	0.0104	0.0092
	(1.1931)	(1.9777)	(1.4096)	(1.7097)
r_{t-2}^{MEX}	0.0151	0.0176	0.0160	0.0163
	(1.8699)	(3.1404)	(2.3488)	(2.9157)
r_{t-3}^{MEX}	0.0098	0.0122	0.0041	0.0061
	(1.2318)	(2.3114)	(0.5612)	(1.1525)

Table 7.1. Continued

Panel 2. The BEKK-GARCH(1,1) Model : The Variance-Covariance Equations

Parameter	Normal Distribution		*t*-Distribution	
	Symmetric	Asymmetric	Symmetric	Asymmetric
c_{11}	0.0741	0.0839	-0.0440	0.0541
	(4.6375)	(5.6855)	3.4516	(4.3695)
c_{21}	0.1265	0.0905	-0.0992	0.0586
	(3.6008)	(3.4166)	2.6015	(2.1608)
c_{22}	0.1614	0.1761	0.1423	0.1746
	(4.0133)	(10.7620)	(6.3501)	(10.2424)
c_{31}	0.0540	0.0395	-0.0411	0.0148
	(3.0602)	(3.0052)	2.8563	(0.9307)
c_{32}	0.0122	0.0199	0.0052	0.0156
	(1.1813)	(1.9856)	(0.4863)	(1.4267)
c_{33}	0.0447	0.0505	0.0511	0.0539
	(3.0040)	(4.0375)	(5.5876)	(5.4162)
a_{11}	0.1850	0.0873	0.1449	0.0775
	(5.5379)	(3.0564)	(8.5845)	(3.6122)
a_{12}	-0.0447	-0.1286	-0.0906	-0.1293
	(0.8756)	(3.9561)	(3.2977)	(4.1822)
a_{13}	0.0307	-0.0324	-0.0081	-0.0389
	0.8519	(1.4093)	(0.5124)	(2.4181)
a_{21}	0.0134	0.0014	0.0100	0.0011
	(1.5194)	(0.2859)	(1.7861)	(0.1628)
a_{22}	0.2943	0.1710	0.2579	0.1677
	(6.0293)	(12.7758)	(11.9926)	(10.8424)
a_{23}	0.0074	-0.0069	0.0020	-0.0033
	0.6728	(1.3085)	(0.3213)	(0.4744)
a_{31}	0.0530	0.0903	0.0596	0.0895
	(0.0530)	(0.0903)	(0.0596)	(0.0895)
a_{32}	0.0642	0.1863	0.0980	0.1816
	(0.0642)	(0.1863)	(0.0980)	(0.1816)
a_{33}	0.1969	0.2772	0.2121	0.2629
	(4.6661)	(6.4586)	(11.6884)	(12.9770)

Table 7.1. Continued

Parameter	Normal Distribution		*t*-Distribution	
	Symmetric	Asymmetric	Symmetric	Asymmetric
b_{11}	0.9800	0.9760	0.9891	0.9830
	(126.4601)	(122.1161)	(294.6741)	(222.5317)
b_{12}	0.0103	0.0145	0.0172	0.0185
	(0.7339)	(1.6027)	(2.9121)	(2.4392)
b_{13}	-0.0060	-0.0041	0.0021	0.0008
	0.7869	(0.5767)	(0.6462)	(0.2043)
b_{21}	-0.0046	-0.0048	-0.0029	-0.0033
	(1.7867)	(2.6696)	(2.0689)	(2.0507)
b_{22}	0.9478	0.9470	0.9588	0.9512
	(53.0703)	(291.6405)	(142.0247)	(207.9020)
b_{23}	-0.0032	-0.0053	-0.0011	-0.0032
	(1.0400)	(3.2185)	(0.7006)	(1.7769)
b_{31}	-0.0081	-0.0095	-0.0104	-0.0101
	(0.9790)	(0.9217)	(2.6446)	(1.7049)
b_{32}	-0.0088	-0.0246	-0.0161	-0.0225
	(0.5205)	(1.5894)	(1.9645)	(1.9937)
b_{33}	0.9786	0.9642	0.9745	0.9661
	(89.8161)	(80.6899)	(221.9527)	(167.0360)
g_{11}		0.2901		0.2646
		(9.4779)		(8.6955)
g_{12}		0.0841		0.0575
		(1.4530)		(1.0722)
g_{13}		0.1771		0.1439
		(3.6749)		(4.9775)
g_{21}		0.0216		0.0150
		(2.1952)		(1.7777)
g_{22}		0.3642		0.3389
		(17.0682)		(15.3678)
g_{23}		0.0372		0.0202
		(2.7956)		(2.3013)
g_{31}		-0.0714		-0.0816
		(1.3396)		(2.4720)

Table 7.1. Continued

Panel 2. The BEKK-GARCH(1,1) Model : The Variance-Covariance Equations

Parameter	Normal Distribution		t-Distribution	
	Symmetric	Asymmetric	Symmetric	Asymmetric
g_{32}		-0.1838		-0.1914
		(1.7085)		(3.0486)
g_{33}		-0.0723		-0.0574
		(0.8876)		(1.6681)
υ			8.6801	9.5725
			(16.0696)	(29.6186)

Note: Numbers in parentheses under coefficient estimates equal absolute value of *t*-statistics.

Table 7.2 presents the log-likelihood statistics, AIC, BIC, the Doornik-Hansen (1994) multivariate tests of normality, and the Hosking (1980) multivariate tests of serial dependence in standardized and squared standardized residuals. The multivariate statistics for the standardized residuals prove insignificant at conventional level, indicating the model specification properly addresses the serial correlation problem. The multivariate statistics for the squared standardized residuals, however, prove significant in the standard BEKK specification, but not significant in the asymmetric version. This suggests that only the asymmetric version of the BEKK model adequately describes the first two moments of the returns series. This observation receives further confirmation from the likelihood ratio test.

As the standard BEKK model nests inside the asymmetric BEKK model, we can easily test one against the other using the likelihood ratio test. The results clearly suggest that asymmetric effects importantly affect the conditional covariances between the returns in the North American markets. The likelihood ratio test statistic equals 234 under the normality assumption and 140 under the Student-*t* distribution assumption. Moreover, with the degrees of freedom equal to 9, we soundly reject the null hypothesis at conventional significance levels. Thus, the model specification with asymmetric effects in covariances dominates the standard BEKK model. Furthermore, using the likelihood ratio test, we can reject the normally distributed asymmetric BEKK model in favor of the *t*-distributed asymmetric BEKK model. The likelihood ratio statistic equals 400, which is significant at conventional significance levels. Consequently, we rely on the asymmetric BEKK specification driven by leptokurtic innovations when interpreting our results.

Table 7.2. Multivariate Diagnostics

Statistic	Normal Distribution		*t*-Distribution	
	Symmetric	Asymmetric	Symmetric	Asymmetric
Log of the Likelihood	-14409	-14292	-14162	-14092
Akaike Information Criterion (AIC)	28927	28711	28435	28313
Schwarz Information Criterion (BIC)	29264	29104	28778	28712
Multivariate Q(12)[a]	115.05	109.31	114.77	110.45
	[0.3032]	[0.4466]	[0.3095]	[0.4165]
Multivariate Q(24)[a]	228.82	223.58	229.49	224.71
	[0.2620]	[0.3473]	[0.2521]	[0.3280]
Multivariate $Q^2(12)$[a]	162.85	116.34	201.05	108.99
	[0.0005]	[0.2747]	[0.0065]	[0.4549]
Multivariate $Q^2(24)$[a]	273.00	243.00	254.89	230.36
	[0.0052]	[0.0975]	[0.0359]	[0.2394]
Multivariate Normality[b]	895	755	1076	874
	[0.0000]	[0.0000]	[0.0000]	[0.0000]

Note: Numbers in brackets equal *p*-values. Numbers in parentheses equal lags.

a. Hosking (1980) multivariate tests for autocorrelation in standardized and squared standardized residuals.

b. Doornik-Hansen (1994) multivariate normality test.

We also consider various conditional volatility models to compare with the BEKK specification. They include the Diagonal VECH model of Bollerslev et al. (1988), the CCC model of Bollerslev (1990), the DCC model of Engle (2002), the VARMA-GARCH model of Ling and McAleer (2003), and the VARMA-AGARCH model of McAleer et al. (2008). We estimate the latter two models using both the CCC specification and the DCC specification. We do not report the full estimation results for economy of space, but in Table 7.3, we present the maximized log-likelihood (under the normal and the *t*-distribution) and the AIC and BIC of the estimated models.

Table 7.3. Alternative Conditional Volatility Models

Model	AIC	BIC	Log-likelihood
Normal Distribution			
Diagonal VECH	28893	29193	-14399
CCC	29218	29480	-14567
CCC VARMA-GARCH	29169	29506	-14531
CCC VARMA -AGARCH	29016	29409	-14445
DCC	28858	29114	-14388
DCC VARMA-GARCH	28853	29184	-14374
DCC VARMA-AGARCH	28733	29119	-14304
t-Distribution			
DIAG VECH	28406	28712	-14154
CCC	28676	28944	-14295
CCC VARMA-GARCH	28642	28985	-14266
CC VARMA-AGARCH	28549	28948	-14211
DCC	28394	28656	-14155
DCC VARMA-GARCH	28390	28727	-14141
DCC VARMA-AGARCH	28316	28709	-14095

Note: The various conditional volatility models that we compare with the BEKK specification include the Diagonal VECH model of Bollerslev et al. (1988), the CCC model of Bollerslev (1990), the DCC model of Engle (2002), the VARMA-GARCH model of Ling and McAleer (2003), and the VARMA-AGARCH model of Chan et al. (2002). We estimate the latter two models using both the CCC specification and the DCC specification.

Interestingly, we reject the null hypothesis of independent conditional means and independent conditional variances of the three returns series. The LR test for the hypothesis that all off-diagonal elements of the A, B, and G matrices equal zero is 3110.77. The likelihood ratio test for the hypothesis that all off-diagonal elements of Γ_1, Γ_2, and Γ_3 equal zero is 55.76. The likelihood ratio that all off-diagonal elements of Γ_1, Γ_2, and Γ_3 and A, B, and G equal zero is 3150.59. Thus, we model the three return series simultaneously (i.e., the asymmetric BEKK version with multivariate t-distribution dominates the separate sequence of three univariate asymmetric t-distributed GARCH models).

From Table 7.1, Panel 1, the following observations emerge. First, we can predict the returns, which reflect their own past returns. The returns of the US and the Mexican indices depend upon their own first two lags, while the returns of the Canadian index depend upon its own three lags. The Wald test statistics that all own lagged returns equal zero are 16.4141 for the US market, 106.7191 for the Mexican market, and 44.5410 for the Canadian market, all significant at the 1-percent level. Predictable returns may reflect market imperfections, time-varying risk premiums, or irrational behavior in markets. Second, no evidence exists of return spillovers from the Mexican stock market to the US stock market. The Wald test statistics for the null hypothesis that all lagged Mexican returns in the US return equation equal zero is 1.5156. Evidence does exist at the 1-percent level, however, of return spillovers from the Mexican stock market to the Canadian stock market, and *vice versa*, at the five-percent level. The Wald test statistic for the null hypothesis that all lagged Mexican returns in the Canadian return equation equal zero is 11.8726 and that all lagged Canadian returns in the Mexican return equation equal zero is 8.8090, rejecting the null hypotheses at the one- and five-percent levels. Similarly, evidence of return spillovers also exists from the Canadian stock market to the US stock market at the five-percent level, and *vice versa*, at the 1-percent level. The Wald test statistic for the null hypothesis that all lagged Canadian returns in the US return equation equal zero is 9.1355 and that all lagged US returns in the Canadian return equation are zero is 52.3494, rejecting the null hypotheses at the 5- and 1 percent levels. Overall, the US and Mexican markets prove relatively more isolated, in terms of returns spillovers, than the US and Canadian markets or even the Canadian and Mexican markets.

The characteristics of the time-varying variance-covariance H_t reflect the A, B, and G matrices. We focus our attention on the results of the estimation of the t-distributed asymmetric BEKK. We make the following observations. First, our results show significant volatility transmission between the second moments of NAFTA stock markets. We reject the null hypothesis at the 1-percent level that the cross-variance effects between the US and Mexico equals zero (i.e., $a_{12}=a_{21}=b_{12}=b_{21}=g_{12}=g_{21}$), using the Wald test. Similarly, we reject the null hypotheses at the 1-percent levels that the cross-variance effects between the US and Canada equal zero (i.e., $a_{13}=a_{31}=b_{13}=b_{31}=g_{13}=g_{31}$), and that that the cross-variance effects between Canada and Mexico equal zero (i.e., $a_{23}=a_{32}=b_{23}=b_{32}=g_{23}=g_{32}$).

Second, the diagonal elements of the *A*, *B*, and *G* matrices prove highly significant (g_{33}, the exception), which implies that volatility in returns responds to its own past shocks and volatility. The exception (i.e., an insignificant g_{33}) implies no asymmetry of the Canadian conditional variance driven by the sign of the error term in the Canadian return equation.

Kearney and Patton (2000) observe, however, that we cannot interpret the estimated parameters c_{ij}, a_{ij}, b_{ij} and g_{ij} for all i , j = 1, 2, 3 individually. The relevant parameters involve nonlinear functions of the original parameters c_{ij}, a_{ij}, b_{ij}, and g_{ij} to generate the constant terms and coefficients of the lagged conditional variances and covariances, lagged squared and cross residuals, lagged squared asymmetric shocks and cross-asymmetric shocks. Statistical inference requires obtaining the first two moments of these nonlinear functions (i.e., the expected value and the standard error of the non-linear combinations of c_{ij}, a_{ij}, b_{ij}, and g_{ij}). We compute the expected value of a non-linear function of random variables as the function of the expected value of the variables, under the assumption of unbiased estimated parameters. Since we use the ML approach to estimate, the consistent ML estimates exhibit a useful property. To wit, if $\hat{\beta}_{MLE}$ consistently estimates β, then $h(\hat{\beta}_{MLE})$ consistently estimates $h(\beta)$. Hence, to produce a consistent estimate of, say a_{ij}^2, we simply square the ML estimate of a_{ij}. To calculate the standard errors of this non-linear function, we apply the delta method and use a first-order Taylor approximation, which yields an approximate formulation of the variance of the non linear functions under fairly general assumptions (Oehlert, 1992).

Table 7.4 displays the linearized parameter estimates for the *t*-distributed asymmetric BEKK model. In Panels 1 and 2, we report the estimates of the three variance equations and the estimates of the covariance equations, respectively. Once again, US = 1, Mexico = 2, and Canada = 3. Hence, h_{11}, h_{22}, and h_{33} denote the conditional variance for the US, Mexican, and Canadian equity return series, respectively, while h_{12}, h_{13}, and h_{23} denote the conditional covariance between the US and Mexican, the US and Canadian, and the Mexican and Canadian equity returns series.

Table 7.4. Linearized Parameter Estimates of the *t*-Distributed Asymmetric BEKK Model

Panel 1: Estimates of the Variance Equations

Variable	h_{11} (S&P500)	h_{22} (IPC)	h_{33} (S&P500/TSX)
constant	0.0368	0.0307	0.0029
	(5.7821)	(5.1952)	(2.7081)
$\varepsilon^2_{1,t-1}$	0.0060	0.0167	0.0015
	(1.8061)	(2.0911)	(1.2090)
$\varepsilon^2_{2,t-1}$	0.0000	0.0281	0.0000
	(0.0814)	(5.4212)	(0.2372)
$\varepsilon^2_{3,t-1}$	0.0080	0.0330	0.0691
	(2.0553)	(2.3184)	(6.4885)
$\varepsilon_{1,t-1}\varepsilon_{2,t-1}$	0.0002	-0.0434	0.0003
	(0.1652)	(3.6000)	(0.4864)
$\varepsilon_{1,t-1}\varepsilon_{3,t-1}$	0.0139	-0.0470	-0.0205
	(4.4817)	(2.4759)	(2.1815)
$\varepsilon_{2,t-1}\varepsilon_{3,t-1}$	0.0002	0.0609	-0.0018
	(0.1628)	(4.5562)	(0.4699)
$h_{11,t-1}$	0.9663	0.0003	0.0000
	(111.2659)	(1.2196)	(0.1022)
$h_{22,t-1}$	0.0000	0.9048	0.0000
	(1.0253)	(103.9510)	(0.8884)
$h_{33,t-1}$	0.0001	0.0005	0.9334
	(0.8524)	(0.9969)	(83.5180)
$h_{12,t-1}$	-0.0064	0.0352	0.0000
	(2.0453)	(2.4511)	(0.1899)
$\varepsilon_{1,t-1}\varepsilon_{2,t-1}$	0.0002	-0.0434	0.0003
	(0.1652)	(3.6000)	(0.4864)
$\varepsilon_{1,t-1}\varepsilon_{3,t-1}$	0.0139	-0.0470	-0.0205
	(4.4817)	(2.4759)	(2.1815)
$\varepsilon_{2,t-1}\varepsilon_{3,t-1}$	0.0002	0.0609	-0.0018
	(0.1628)	(4.5562)	(0.4699)

Table 7.4. Continued

Panel 1: Estimates of the Variance Equations

Variable	h_{11} (S&P500)	h_{22} (IPC)	h_{33} (S&P500/TSX)
$h_{11,t-1}$	0.9663	0.0003	0.0000
	(111.2659)	(1.2196)	(0.1022)
$h_{22,t-1}$	0.0000	0.9048	0.0000
	(1.0253)	(103.9510)	(0.8884)
$h_{33,t-1}$	0.0001	0.0005	0.9334
	(0.8524)	(0.9969)	(83.5180)
$h_{12,t-1}$	-0.0064	0.0352	0.0000
	(2.0453)	(2.4511)	(0.1899)
$h_{13,t-1}$	-0.0198	-0.0428	0.0016
	(1.6957)	(1.9931)	(0.2045)
$h_{23,t-1}$	0.0001	-0.0428	-0.0062
	(1.3317)	(1.9931)	(1.7757)
$\eta^2_{1,t-1}$	0.0700	0.0033	0.0207
	(4.3477)	(0.5361)	(2.4887)
$\eta^2_{2,t-1}$	0.0002	0.1148	0.0004
	(0.8888)	(7.6839)	(1.1507)
$\eta^2_{3,t-1}$	0.0067	0.0366	0.0033
	(1.2360)	(1.5243)	(0.8341)
$\eta_{1,t-1}\eta_{2,t-1}$	0.0079	0.0390	0.0058
	(1.8047)	(1.0940)	(2.2594)
$\eta_{1,t-1}\eta_{3,t-1}$	-0.0432	-0.0220	-0.0165
	(2.0000)	(0.8319)	(1.3141)
$\eta_{2,t-1}\eta_{3,t-1}$	-0.0024	-0.1297	-0.0023
	(1.4064)	(2.9789)	(1.2777)

Table 7.4. (Continued)

Panel 2: Estimates of the Covariance Equations

Variable	h_{12} (S&P500 and IPC)	h_{13} (S&P500 and S&P500/TSX)	h_{23} (IPC and S&P500/TSX)
constant	0.0105	0.0008	0.0008
	(2.2352)	(0.8769)	(1.3477)
$\varepsilon^2_{1,t-1}$	-0.0100	-0.0030	0.0050
	(4.4107)	(3.0649)	(1.7363)
$\varepsilon^2_{2,t-1}$	0.0002	0.0000	-0.0006
	(0.1623)	(0.1672)	(0.4768)
$\varepsilon^2_{3,t-1}$	0.0163	0.0235	0.0477
	(2.3280)	(3.2653)	(3.6607)
$\varepsilon_{1,t-1}\varepsilon_{2,t-1}$	0.0129	0.0000	-0.0061
	(3.1911)	(0.5699)	(1.9351)
$\varepsilon_{1,t-1}\varepsilon_{3,t-1}$	0.0025	0.0169	-0.0411
	(0.3914)	(2.6124)	(3.3080)
$\varepsilon_{2,t-1}\varepsilon_{3,t-1}$	0.0152	0.0000	0.0435
	(3.7464)	(0.0090)	(8.3048)
$h_{11,t-1}$	0.0182	0.0008	0.0003
	(2.4199)	(0.2042)	(1.2196)
$h_{22,t-1}$	-0.0031	0.0000	-0.0031
	(2.0529)	(1.1554)	(1.7779)
$h_{33,t-1}$	0.0002	0.0097	-0.0218
	(0.9796)	(1.7192)	(2.0109)
$h_{12,t-1}$	0.9350	-0.0032	0.0007
	(159.4208)	(1.7733)	(0.1899)
$h_{13,t-1}$	-0.0223	0.9497	0.0147
	(1.9766)	(196.9415)	(2.0380)
$h_{23,t-1}$	-0.0095	-0.0031	0.9191
	(1.7009)	(2.0365)	(130.5956)
$\eta^2_{1,t-1}$	0.0152	0.0381	0.0083
	(0.9765)	(3.3697)	(0.9240)

Table 7.4. (Continued)

Panel 2: Estimates of the Covariance Equations

Variable	h_{12} (S&P500 and IPC)	h_{13} (S&P500 and S&P500/TSX)	h_{23} (IPC and S&P500/TSX)
$\eta^2_{2,t-1}$	0.0051	0.0003	0.0068
	(1.7402)	(1.1928)	(2.2689)
$\eta^2_{3,t-1}$	0.0156	0.0047	0.0110
	(1.4299)	(1.0587)	(1.1487)
$\eta_{1,t-1}\eta_{2,t-1}$	0.0905	0.0075	0.0499
	(7.8369)	(2.4718)	(4.5962)
$\eta_{1,t-1}\eta_{3,t-1}$	-0.0424	-0.0269	-0.0308
	(2.9821)	(1.6586)	(1.7717)
$\eta_{2,t-1}\eta_{3,t-1}$	-0.0305	-0.0025	-0.0233
	(2.5262)	(1.6149)	(1.8083)

Note: Numbers in parentheses under coefficient estimates equal t-statistics.

An analysis of the results requires a preliminary taxonomy of the transmission channels. We can visualize two transmission channels. First, consider the transmission of volatility, which includes a) a direct volatility transmission, where $h_{ii,t}$ responds to $h_{ii,t-1}$ (its own volatility) and/or to $h_{jj,t-1}$ (volatility in the other markets) and b) an indirect volatility transmission, where $h_{ii,t}$ responds to any covariance $h_{ij,t-1}$, for $i \neq j$, i and j = 1 ,2, 3. Second, consider now the transmission of shocks, which includes a) a direct shock transmission, where $h_{ii,t}$ responds to $\varepsilon^2_{ii,t-1}$ (its own shock) and/or to $\varepsilon^2_{jj,t-1}$ (shock in the other markets) and b) an indirect shock transmission, where $h_{ii,t}$ responds to any of the cross terms $\varepsilon_{i,t-1}\varepsilon_{j,t-1}$ for $i \neq j$, i and j = 1, 2, 3.

The results indicate that the conditional variance of US returns responds directly to its own past volatility and its own past shocks as well as to past shocks originating from the Canadian market. Volatility and shocks from the Mexican market do not significantly affect the conditional variance of US returns. US returns exhibit own-variance asymmetry, cross-variance asymmetry, and covariance asymmetry. Shocks originating in the US market prove asymmetric, given the significance of the coefficient on $\eta^2_{1,t-1}$. That is, negative shocks in the US market increase the volatility of US returns more than 12 times than positive shocks (i.e., 0.076 versus 0.006). Positive and negative shocks originating in the Canadian markets do not affect the volatility of US returns asymmetrically, however. In addition, the conditional variance of the US returns displays indirectly cross-variance asymmetry with respect to shocks in the Canadian market, given the significance of the coefficients on the cross term $\varepsilon_{1,t-1}\varepsilon_{3,t-1}$ and its corresponding asymmetric term $\eta_{1,t-1}\eta_{3,t-1}$. Finally, the volatility of US returns also exhibit own- and cross-covariance asymmetry, as the coefficients on $\eta_{1,t-1}\eta_{2,t-1}$ and $\eta_{1,t-1}\eta_{3,t-1}$ as well as $\eta_{2,t-1}\eta_{3,t-1}$ prove significant in the covariance equation, respectively.

The behavior of the Mexican market volatility differs substantially from that of the US market. The volatility of the Mexican returns responds directly to both its own past shocks and its own past volatility. Further, while the conditional variances of US and Canadian returns do not directly affect the volatility of the Mexican returns, shocks originating in the US and Canadian markets directly affect the volatility of Mexican returns. This finding implies that a mechanism exists that directly transmits shocks from the US and the Canadian markets to the Mexican market, which we conjecture may reflect US and Canadian investors operating in the Mexican market. Furthermore, all the coefficients on the covariance and cross-shocks terms prove significant. This implies that an indirect mechanism also exists for volatility and shock transmission from the US and Canadian markets to the Mexican market. Mexican returns also exhibit own-variance asymmetry, as indicated by the significance of the coefficient on $\eta^2_{2,t-1}$. The effect of negative shocks equals about 8 times the effect of positive shocks (i.e., 0.1429 versus 0.0167). Mexican returns also exhibit cross-variance asymmetry, through the Mexican and Canadian cross-shocks term $\eta_{2,t-1}\eta_{3,t-1}$, and own- and cross-covariance asymmetry. The latter effect emerges, since the coefficient estimates of $\eta_{1,t-1}\eta_{2,t-1}$ and $\eta_{1,t-1}\eta_{3,t-1}$ as well as $\eta_{2,t-1}\eta_{3,t-1}$ prove significant in the covariance equation between US and Mexican returns (the h_{12} equation) and the parameter estimates of $\eta_{1,t-1}$ $\eta_{2,t-1}$ and $\eta^2_{2,t-1}$ prove significant in the covariance equation between Canadian and Mexican returns (the h_{23} equation).

The results for the Canadian market indicate that Canadian returns respond directly to their own past shocks and their own past volatility. No evidence emerges, however, of own-variance asymmetry. Instead, evidence exists of cross-variance asymmetry through the significance of the US shock term $\eta_{1,t-1}^2$ and the US and Mexican cross-shock term $\eta_{1,t-1}\eta_{2,t-1}$. Some evidence also exists of cross-, but not own-, covariance asymmetry, as the parameter estimates of $\eta_{2,t-1}^2$ and $\eta_{1,t-1}\eta_{2,t-1}$ prove significant in the covariance equation between Canadian and Mexican returns (the h_{23} equation), and the parameter estimate of $\eta_{1,t-1}^2$ and $\eta_{1,t-1}\eta_{2,t-1}$ prove significant in the covariance equation between US and Canadian returns (the h_{13} equation).

Table 7.5 reports the parameter estimates of negative shocks on the variances and covariances of returns (e.g., the effect of $\varepsilon_{1,t-1}^2$ on $h_{11,t}$ equals a_{11}^2 for $\varepsilon_{1,t-1} > 0$, and $a_{11}^2 + g_{11}$ for $\varepsilon_{1,t-1} < 0$).

Table 7.5. Parameter Estimates of Negative Shocks

Panel 1: The Variance Equations

Variable	h_{11}	h_{22}	h_{33}
$\varepsilon_{1,t-1}^2$ for $\varepsilon_{1,t-1} < 0$.	0.0760 (4.8692)	0.0200 (1.7955)	0.0222 (2.6056)
$\varepsilon_{2,t-1}^2$ for $\varepsilon_{2,t-1} < 0$.	0.0002 (0.8933)	0.1429 (9.0194)	.0004 (1.1607)
$\varepsilon_{3,t-1}^2$ for $\varepsilon_{3,t-1} < 0$.	0.0147 (1.9036)	0.0696 (2.1526)	0.0724 (5.9771)
$\varepsilon_{1,t-1}\varepsilon_{2,t-1}$, for $\varepsilon_{1,t-1}\varepsilon_{2,t-1} < 0$.	0.0081 (1.8148)	-0.0044 (0.1255)	0.0061 (2.2711)
$\varepsilon_{1,t-1}\varepsilon_{3,t-1}$ for $\varepsilon_{1,t-1}\varepsilon_{3,t-1} < 0$.	-0.0293 (1.3386)	-0.0690 (1.8713)	-0.0370 (2.2151)

Table 7.5. Continued

Panel 1: The Variance Equations

Variable	h_{11}	h_{22}	h_{33}
$\varepsilon_{2,t-1}\varepsilon_{3,t-1}$ for $\varepsilon_{2,t-1}\varepsilon_{3,t-1} < 0$.	-0.0022 (1.0520)	-0.0688 (1.7237)	-0.0041 (0.9570)
$\varepsilon^2_{1,t-1}$ for $\varepsilon_{1,t-1} < 0$.	0.0052 (0.3309)	0.0351 (3.1248)	0.0133 (1.3261)
$\varepsilon^2_{2,t-1}$ for $\varepsilon_{2,t-1} < 0$.	0.0052 (1.7025)	0.0003 (1.1815)	0.0063 (1.9852)
$\varepsilon^2_{3,t-1}$ for $\varepsilon_{3,t-1} < 0$.	0.0319 (2.0953)	0.0282 (2.9525)	0.0587 (3.1186)
$\varepsilon_{1,t-1}\varepsilon_{2,t-1}$ for $\varepsilon_{1,t-1}\varepsilon_{2,t-1} < 0$.	0.1034 (9.1143)	0.0075 (2.3621)	0.0438 (4.0146)
$\varepsilon_{1,t-1}\varepsilon_{3,t-1}$ for $\varepsilon_{1,t-1}\varepsilon_{3,t-1} < 0$.	0.0930 (8.2781)	-0.0100 (0.5420)	-0.0719 (2.9203)
$\varepsilon_{2,t-1}\varepsilon_{3,t-1}$ for $\varepsilon_{2,t-1}\varepsilon_{3,t-1} < 0$.	-0.0153 (1.3411)	-0.0025 (1.0045)	0.0202 (1.5279)

Note: Numbers in parentheses under coefficient estimates equal absolute values of *t*-statistics.

Figures 7.1 and 7.2 present the plots of the respective conditional variances for the US, Mexican, and Canadian equity markets return series and the conditional covariances, implied by the estimates of the t-distributed asymmetric BEKK model, respectively. Clearly, the variances and covariances cluster over time. The conditional variances and covariances do not remain constant over time and appear especially volatile between 1997 and 2003 (Asian financial crisis and stock-market crash). The Mexican market also exhibited high volatility of the conditional variance between 1994 and 1995 (Peso crisis). Volatilities move together. Covariances between any two of the three returns are higher (lower) in times of high (low) volatility and include, in some instances, large positive spikes.

Conditional Variance S&P500 1992 -2007

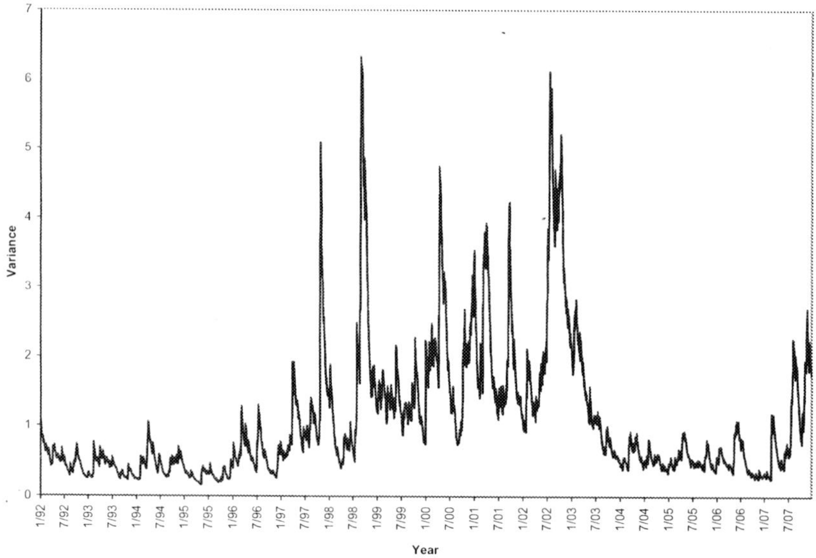

Conditional Variance IPC 1992 -2007

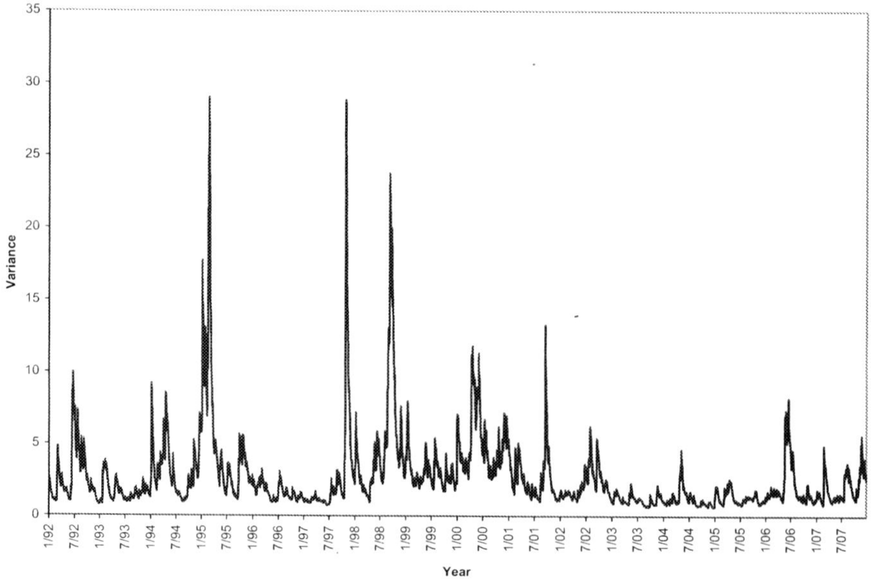

Conditional Variance S&P/TSX 1992 -2007

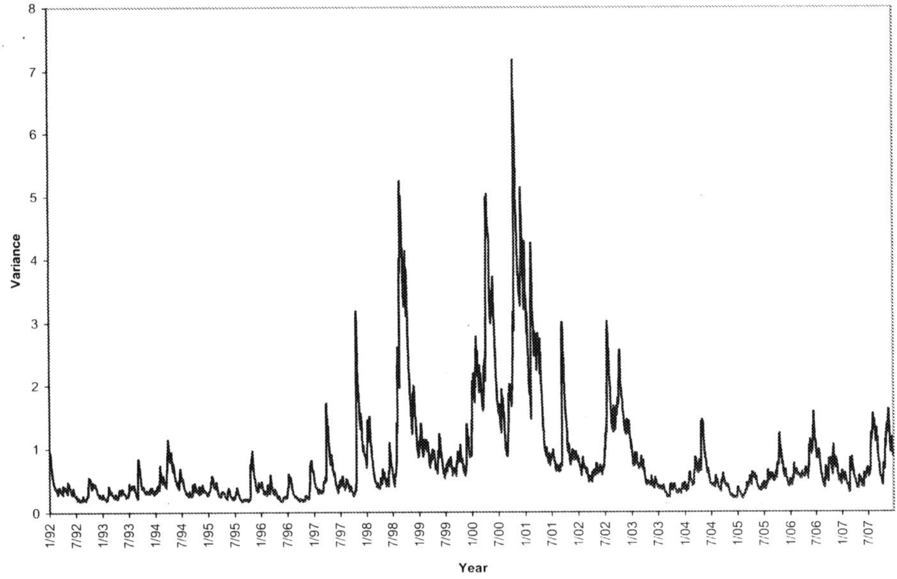

Figure 7.1. Conditional Variances.

Conditional Covariance S&P 500 and IPC 1992 -2007

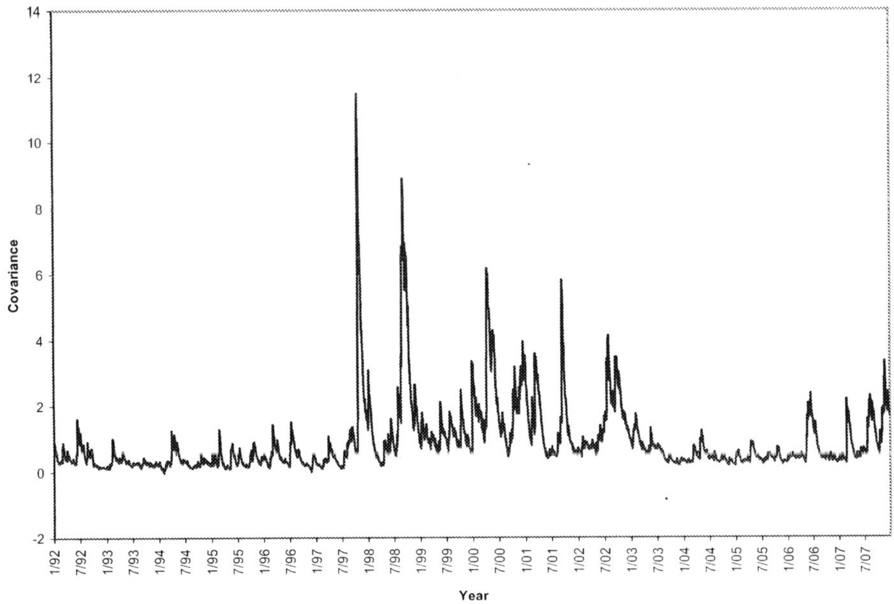

Conditional Covariance S&P 500 and S&P/TSX 1992 -2007

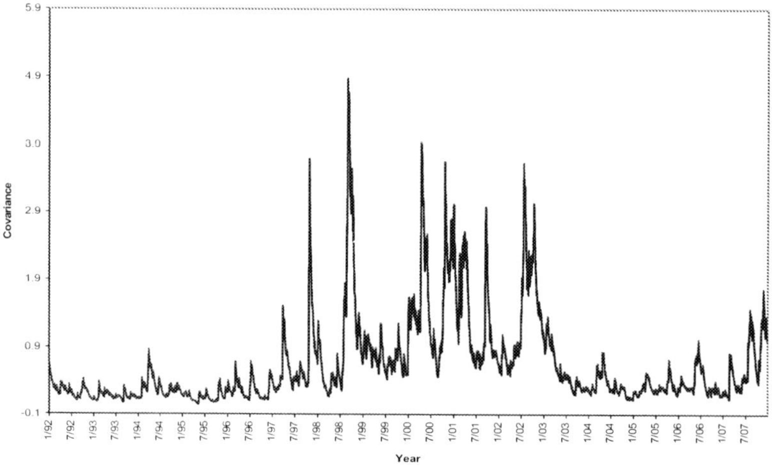

Conditional Covariance IPC and SP/TSX 1992 -2007

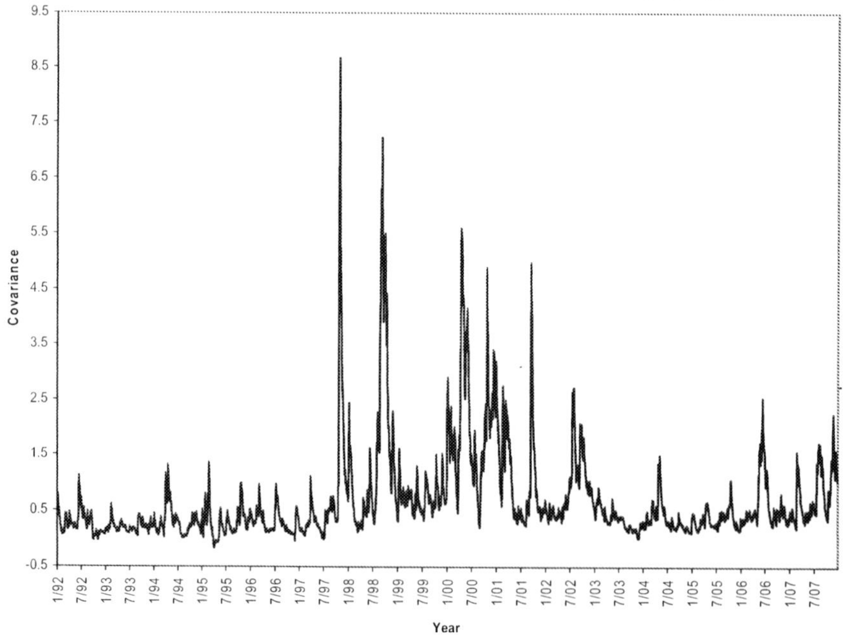

Figure 7.2. Conditional Covariances.

Previous studies suggest that correlations vary over time and that they increased since the mid-1990s due to wider financial integration (Bekaert and Harvey, 1997, 2002). Following De Goeji and Marquering (2004), we examine whether the time variability in covariances is only due to the variation in variances. The conditional correlation coefficient $\rho_{ij,t}$ between return *i* and return *j* at time *t* is defined as follows:

$$\rho_{ij,t} = \frac{cov(r_{i,t}, r_{j,t})}{\sqrt{var(r_{i,t})}\sqrt{var(r_{j,t})}}. \tag{7.1}$$

If $\rho_{ij,t}$ does not change over time, then the covariance's variability exclusively reflects the variances' variations. As such, modeling of time-varying covariance proves uninteresting, as the variances capture all the dynamics.

Conditional Correlations: S&P500 and IPC 1992 -2007

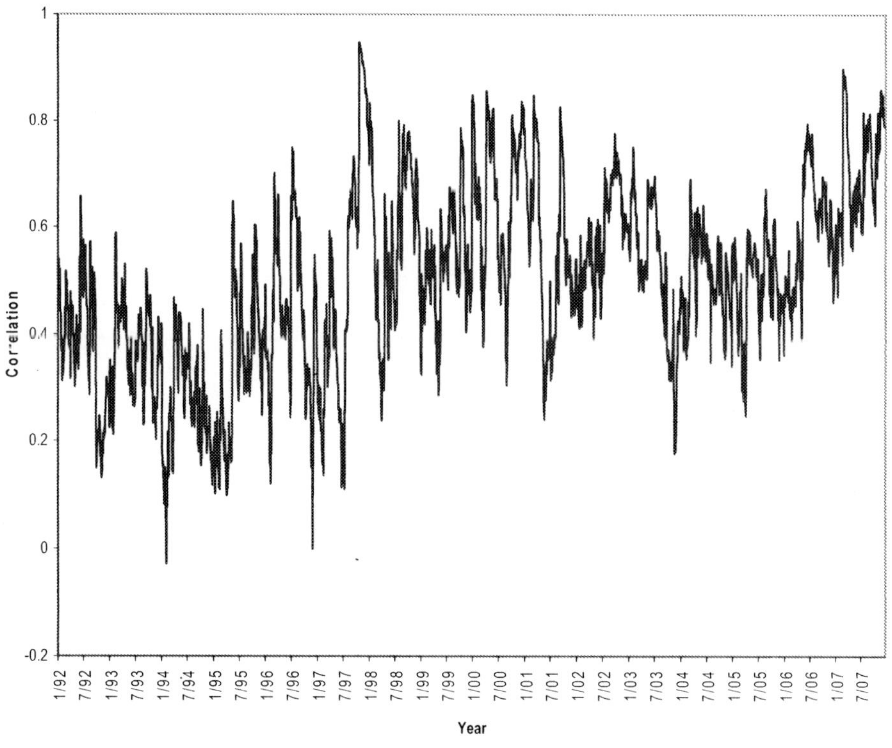

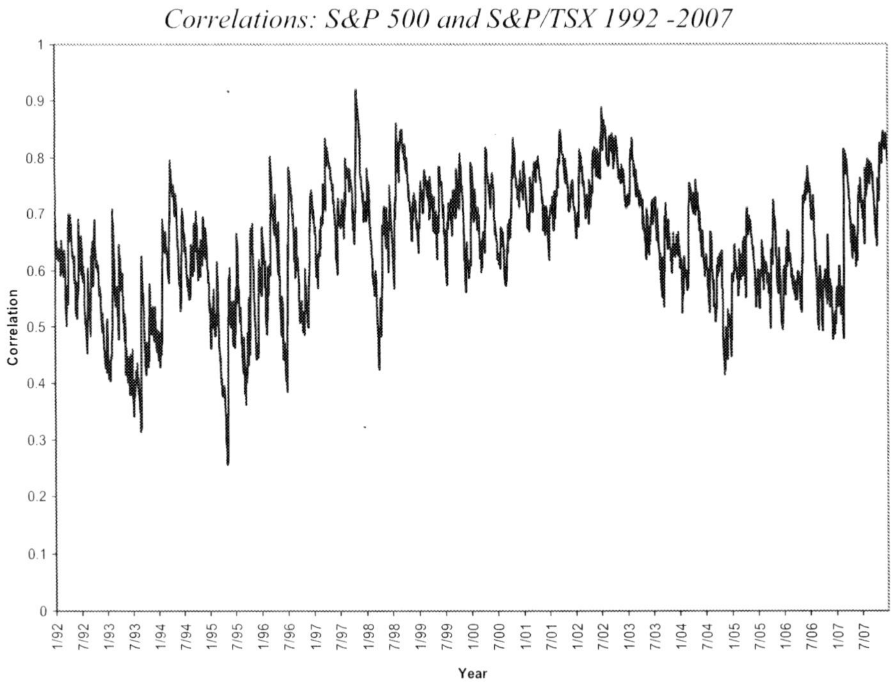

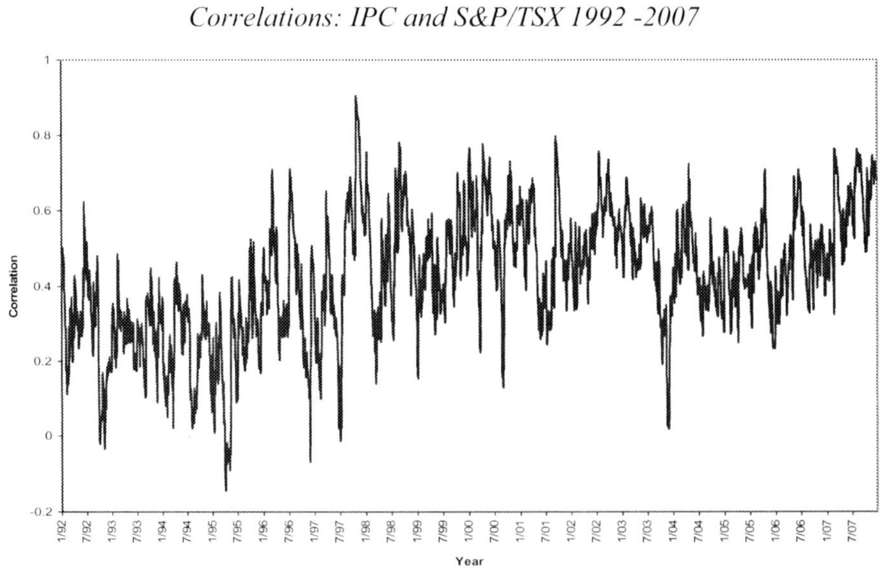

Figure 7.3. Conditional Correlations.

Figure 7.3 displays the evolution of the estimated conditional correlation coefficients. The plots of the series appear to refute a constant conditional correlation, as considerable variability occurs over time. More trend, however, appears when we include the Mexican market. That is, the correlations between the US and Canadian markets seem to rise from 0.6 to 0.8 over the sample period, whereas the correlations between the Mexican and the US or Canadian markets appear to rise from 0.4 to 0.8 and from 0.2 to 0.6, respectively. A formal test of the constancy of the correlation coefficients regresses the conditional correlation coefficients on a constant and lagged conditional correlation coefficients, rejecting the hypotheses of constant correlation coefficients. The estimates on the lagged conditional correlation coefficients prove significantly different from zero, with *t*-ratios equal to, respectively, 274.8890 (S&P500 and IPC), 287.0184 (S&P500 and S&P/TSX), and 249.7295 (IPC and S&P/TSX).

We can draw some observations about the estimated conditional correlation coefficients. First, the conditional correlations between each pair of returns, on average, are positive. The mean values equal 0.4994 (S&P500 and IPC), 0.6460 (S&P500 and S&P/TSX), and 0.4274 (IPC and S&P/TSX) and their associated standard errors equal 0.0028, 0.0018, and 0.0027, respectively. A simple *t* test concludes that these values significantly differ from zero. Second, the conditional correlations between the returns show large variations during episodes of financial crisis. Kaminsky and Reinhart (2000) suggest that these rapid and sharp movements in correlations make the financial market a potential channel of contagion. Third, the magnitude of the conditional correlations indicates that in the last few years, the Mexican stock market became more integrated with the US and Canadian markets. In the early 1990s, the conditional correlations between the US and Mexican stock markets follow a downward trend, and show an average value of about 0.4. Now, in the early 2000s, we observe an upward trend and with average value of about 0.6. We see the same pattern, although with a smaller magnitude, in the evolution of the conditional correlations between the Mexican and the Canadian markets.

Chapter 8

CONCLUSION

This study explores the first- and second-moment interactions among the NAFTA stock markets, using daily data over the period 1992-2007. We focus the analysis on three issues. First, we examine the long-run relationships between the markets. Second, we consider the short-run relationship between them. And, third, we investigate the return and volatility transmission process between them.

We address the first issue using the standard cointegration techniques of Johansen and Juselius (1990) and the recursive cointegration techniques of Hansen and Johansen (1999). Standard cointegration analysis fails to discover evidence that the NAFTA stock indices share long run equilibrium relationships. We do not reverse these findings with the recursive cointegration analysis. These latter finding show a strengthening of the relationships between the three markets in the mid-nineties, as the NAFTA markets appear to move toward cointegration. This movement, however, reverses by the end of the 1990s. In general, the results of the recursive cointegration tests prove compatible with the traditional cointegration findings. We conclude, therefore, that no evidence exists of a common long-term trend between the three NAFTA equity indices, and no evidence exists of any move toward such a trend relationship.

We address the second issue with the generalized impulse-response analysis of Pesaran and Shin (1998). We find that the responses prove large in scale, using the conventional 0.20 unit standard deviations definition of significant responses on stock returns. The responses occur immediately, but do not exhibit long-lasting effects. In all cases, the responses die out within two days. We also find that the response of each market to shocks in its own market always exceeds the response to shocks in other markets. The US holds a leading role in that the Canadian (Mexican) market responds more sensitively to shocks stemming from the US than from Mexico (Canada). The generalized impulse responses show, however, that the US market does respond to shocks originating in Mexico and Canada. Hence, the US market leads, but is not autonomous and independent.

We address the third issue by modeling the joint distribution of the three stock returns using a vector autoregression methodology with innovations, using a multivariate asymmetric BEKK-GARCH(1,1) process. We estimate the model under two distributional forms for the innovations – the multivariate normal distribution and the multivariate Student-*t* density. The multivariate normal distribution, the most common and convenient, does not accommodate leptokurtic data, while the multivariate Student-*t* density does. Our preliminary findings, based on LR tests, indicate that the BEKK specification with asymmetric effects in covariances dominates the standard symmetric BEKK model. Furthermore, we reject the normally distributed asymmetric BEKK model in favor of the *t*-distributed asymmetric BEKK model. The asymmetric BEKK results support significant returns and volatility spillovers between the three stock markets. Our results exhibit significant volatility transmission between the first moments of the NAFTA stock markets. Although we find no evidence of return spillovers from the Mexican to the US stock market, we do find evidence of return spillovers from the Mexican to the Canadian stock market, from the Canadian to the US stock market, from the Canadian to the Mexican stock market, and from the US to the Canadian stock market. This evidence suggests that based on the first moments, the US and the Mexican markets prove relatively more isolated than the US and Canadian or even the Canadian and Mexican markets.

Our results also exhibit significant volatility transmission between the second moments of the NAFTA stock markets, albeit not homogenous. US returns exhibit own-variance asymmetry, cross-variance asymmetry, and own- and cross-covariance asymmetry. The conditional variance of US returns responds directly to its own past volatility and shocks as well as to shocks originating in the Canadian market. In contrast, volatility and shocks from the Mexican market do not significantly and directly affect the conditional variance of US returns. The conditional variance of the Mexican returns also responds directly to its own past volatility and shocks. The conditional variance of US and Canadian returns does not directly affect the volatility of the Mexican returns. Shocks originating in the US and Canadian markets, however, directly affect the volatility of the Mexican returns. Mexican returns also exhibit own-variance asymmetry, cross-variance asymmetry, and own- and cross-covariance asymmetry. The conditional variance of Canadian returns also responds directly to its own past volatility and shocks. No evidence exists, however, of own-variance asymmetry. Instead, evidence exists of cross-variance asymmetry and some evidence of cross-, but not own-, covariance asymmetry.

The magnitude and trend of the conditional correlations indicate that in the last few years, the Mexican stock market exhibited a tendency toward increased integration with the US market. In the early 1990s, the conditional correlations between the US and Mexican stock markets followed a downward trend, with an average value of approximately 0.4. Conversely, in the early 2000s, the trend reversed, now rising, with an average value of 0.6. The same pattern, although with slightly lower magnitude, also appears in the evolution of the conditional correlations between the Mexican and the Canadian markets. The finding of volatility transmission between the three NAFTA markets, and the pattern of correlations that emerges, can provide important practical importance to financial market participants and may guide those participants in making optimal portfolio decisions. In the NAFTA stock markets, the benefits of portfolio diversification are not yet exhausted.

Finally, we do note that evidence exists that the Peso and Asian financial crises as well as the stock-market crash in the US affect the return and volatility time-series relationships. Consequently, future empirical work can consider the possibility of one-time structural shifts in the return and volatility relationships, occurring near the Peso and Asian financial crises as well as the US stock-market crash. Accommodating such one-time structural shifts may permit an underlying cointegrating relationship to achieve significance, alter the short run relationships between the NAFTA markets, and affect the return and volatility transmission process.

REFERENCES

Akaike, H., (1974). A look at the statistical model identification. *IEEE Transactions on Automatic Control* AC-19, 716-723.

Akaike, H., (1978).A Bayesian analysis of the minimum AIC procedure. *Annals of the Institute of Statistical Mathematics* 30, 9-14.

Akaike, H., (1979). Bayesian extension of the minimum AIC procedure of autoregressive model fitting. *Biometrika* 66, 237-242.

Adler, M., & Qi, R., (2003). Mexico's integration into the North American capital market. *Emerging Market Review* 4, 91-120.

Aggarwal, R., & Kyaw, N. A., (2005). Equity market integration in the NAFTA region: Evidence from unit root and cointegration tests. *International Review of Financial Analysis* 14, 393-406.

Andrews, D. W. K., (1993). Tests for parameter instability and structural change with unknown change point. *Econometrica* 61: 821-856.

Andrews, D.W.K., & Ploberger, W., (1994). Optimal tests when a nuisance parameter is present only under the alternative. *Econometrica* 62, 1383-1414.

Ang, A., & Bekaert, G., (2002). International asset allocation with regime shifts. *The Review of Financial Studies* 15, 1137-1187.

Ang, A., & Chen, J., (2002). Asymmetric correlations of equity portfolios. *Journal of Financial Economics* 63, 443-494.

Arshanapalli, B., & Doukas, J., (1993). International stock market linkages: Evidence from the pre- and post-October 1987 period. *Journal of Banking and Finance* 17, 193-208.

Arshanspalli, B., Doukas, J., & Lang, L. H. P., (1997). Common volatility in the industrial structure of global capital markets. *Journal of International Money and Finance* 16, 189-209.

Atteberry, W. L., & Swanson, P. E., (1997). Equity market integration: the case of North America. *North American Journal of Economics and Finance* 8, 23-37.

Balke, N. S., & Fomby, T.B., (1997). Threshold cointegration. *International Economic Review* 38, 627-645.

Barndorff -Nielsen, O. E., & Shephard, N., (2004). Power and bipower variation with stochastic volatility and jumps. *Journal of Financial Econometrics* 2, 1-37.

Bauwens, L., & Laurent, S., (2005). A new class of multivariate skew densities with applications to GARCH models. *Journal of Business and Economic Statistics* 23, 346-354.

Bauwens, L., Laurent S., & Rombouts, J. V. K., (2006). Multivariate GARCH models: A survey. *Journal of Applied Econometrics* 21, 79-109.

Bekaert, G., & Harvey, C. R., (1995). Time-varying world market integration. *The Journal of Finance* 50, 403-444.

Bekaert, G., & Harvey, C. R., (1997). Emerging equity market volatility. *Journal of Financial Economics* 43, 29-77.

Bekaert, G., & Harvey, C.R., (2002). Research in Emerging Market Finance: Looking to the Future. *Emerging Markets Review* 3, 429-448.

Bera, A. K., & Higgins, M. L., (1992). A test for conditional heteroskedasticity in time series model. *Journal of Time Series Analysis* 13, 501-519.

Bera, A. K., & Higgins, M. L., (1993). ARCH models: Properties, estimation, and testing. *Journal of Economic Surveys* 7, 305-366.

Black, F., (1976). Studies in price volatility changes. *Proceedings of the 1976 meeting of the business and economics statistics section.* American Statistical Association, 177-181.

Blackman, S. C., Holden, K., & Thomas, W. A., (1994). Long-term relationship between international share prices. *Applied Financial Economics* 4, 297-304

Bollerslev, T., (1986). Generalized autoregressive conditional heteroscedasticity. *Journal of Econometrics* 31, 307-328.

Bollerslev, T., (1987). A conditionally heteroskedastic time series model for speculative prices and rates of return. *Review of Economics and Statistics* 69, 542-547.

Bollerslev, T., (1990). Modelling the coherence in short-run nominal exchange rates: A multivariate generalized ARCH model. *Review of Economics and Statistics* 72, 498-505.

Bollerslev, T., Chou, R. Y., & Kroner, K. F., (1992). ARCH modeling in finance: A review of the theory and empirical evidence. *Journal of Econometrics* 52, 5-59.

Bollerslev, T., Engle, R. F., & Nelson, D. B., (1994). ARCH models. In *Handbook of Econometrics*, vol. 4 (Ed by Engle R. F. & McFadden, D. L.), 2961-3038. North-Holland, Amsterdam.

Bollerslev, T., Engle, R. F., & Wooldridge, J. M., (1988). A capital asset pricing model with time varying covariances. *Journal of Political Economy* 96, 116-131.

Bollerslev, T., & Wooldridge, J. M., (1992). Quasi-maximum likelihood estimation inference in dynamic models with time-varying covariances. *Econometric Theory* 11, 143-172.

Booth, G., Martikainen, T., & Tse, Y., (1997). Price and volatility spillovers in Scandinavian stock markets. *Journal of Banking and Finance* 21, 811-823.

Braun, P. A., Nelson, D. B., & Sunnier, A. M., (1995). Good news, bad news, volatility and betas. *Journal of Finance* 50, 1575-1603.

Brooks, C., & Henry, O. T., (2000). Linear and non-linear transmission of equity return volatility: Evidence from the US, Japan and Australia. *Economic Modelling* 17, 497-513.

Brooks, R., & Del Negro, M., (2004). The rise in comovement across national stock markets: Market integration or IT bubble? *Journal of Empirical Finance* 11, 649-680.

Brooks, R., & Ragunathan, V., (2003). Returns and volatility on the Chinese stock markets. *Applied Financial Economics* 13, 747-752.

Broyden, C. G., (1970). The convergence of a class of double-rank minimization algorithms. *Journal of the Institute of Mathematics and Its Applications* 6, 76-90

Cajigas, J., & Urga, G., (2006). Dynamic conditional correlation models with asymmetric multivariate Laplace innovations. Working Paper, Cass Business School, London.

Campbell, J. Y., & Hentschel, L., (1992). No news is good news: An asymmetric model of changing volatility in stock returns. *Journal of Financial Economics* 31, 281-318.

Campos, J., Ericsson, N. R., & Hendry, D. F., (1996). Cointegration tests in the presence of structural breaks. *Journal of Econometrics* 70, 187-220.

Chang, T., (2001). Are there any long-run benefits from international equity diversification for Taiwan investors diversifying in the equity markets of its major trading partners, Hong Kong, Japan, South Korea, Thailand and the USA. *Applied Economics Letters* 8, 441-446.

Chen, G. M., Firth, M., & Rui, O. M., (2002). Stock market linkages: Evidence from Latin America. *Journal of Banking and Finance* 26, 1113-1141.

Chen, N., & Zhang, F., (1997). Correlations, trades and stock returns of the Pacific-Basin markets. *Pacific-Basin Finance Journal* 5, 559-577.

Cheung, Y.-W., & Lai, K. S., (1993). Finite sample sizes of Johansen's likelihood ratio tests for cointegration. *Oxford Bulletin of Economics and Statistics* 55, 313-328.

Chorhay, A., Tournai, A., & Urbain, J. P., (1993). Common stochastic trends in European stock markets. *Economic Letters* 42, 385-390.

Choudhry, T., (1996). Interdependence of stock markets: Evidence from Europe during the 1920s and 1930s. *Applied Financial Economics* 6, 243-249.

Christie, A., (1982). The stochastic behaviour of common stock variance: value, leverage and interest rate effects. *Journal of Financial Economics* 10, 407-432.

Ciner, C., (2006). A further look at linkages between NAFTA equity markets. *The Quarterly Review of Economics and Finance* 46, 338-352.

Cotter, J., (2004). International equity market integration in a small open economy: Ireland January 1990-December 2000, *International Review of Financial Analysis* 13, 669-685.

Crowder, W. J., & Wohar, M.E., (1998). Cointegration, forecasting and international stock prices. *Global Finance Journal* 9, 181-204.

Daniels, J., & Vanhoose, D. D., (2004). *Global economic issues and policies.* Mason, Ohio: South-Western.

D'Agostino, R. B., (1970). Transformation to normality of the null distribution of g1. *Biometrika* 57, 679-681.

Darrat, A. F., & Zhong, M., (2005). Equity market integration and multinational agreements: The case of NAFTA. *Journal of International Money and Finance* 24, 793-817.

Dekker, A., Sen, K., & Young, M. R., (2001). Equity markets linkages in the Asia Pacific Region: A comparison of the orthogonalized and generalized VAR approach. *Global Finance Journal* 12, 1-33.

Dickey, D. A., & Fuller, W. A., (1979). Distribution of the estimators for autoregressive time series with a unit root. *Journal of the American Statistical Association* 74, 427-431.

Doornik, J. A., & Hansen, H., (1994). An omnibus test for univariate and multivariate normality. Discussion paper, Nuffield College, University of Oxford, Oxford, UK.

Engle, R. F., (1982). Autoregressive conditional heteroskedasticity with estimates of the variance of U.K. inflation. *Econometrica* 50, 987-1008.

Engle, R. F., (2002). Dynamic conditional correlation: A simple class of multivariate GARCH models. *Journal of Business and Economic Statistics* 20, 339-350.

Engle, R. F., & Cho, Y.-H., (1999). Time varying betas and asymmetric effects of news: Empirical analysis of blue chip stocks. NBER Working Paper No. 7330, Cambridge, MA.

Engle, R. F., & Granger, C. W. J., (1987). Co-integration and error correction representation, estimation, and testing. *Econometrica* 55, 251-276.

Engle, R. F., & Kroner, K., (1995). Multivariate simultaneous generalised ARCH. *Econometric Theory* 11, 122-150.

Engle, R. F., & Ng, N., (1993). Measuring and testing the impact of news on volatility. *Journal of Finance* 48, 1749-1778.

Engle, R. F., & Susmel, R., (1993). Common volatility in international equity markets. *Journal of Business* and *Economic Statistics* 11, 167-176.

Eun, C. S., & Shim, S., (1989). International transmission of stock market movements. *Journal of Financial and Quantitative Analysis* 24, 241-256.

Ewing, B. T., Payne, J. E., & Sowell, C., (1999). NAFTA and North American stock market linkages: An empirical note. *North American Journal of Economics and Finance* 10, 443-451.

Ewing, B. T., Payne, J. E., & Sowell, C., (2001). Transmission of conditional stock return volatility across North American markets: Evidence from pre- and post-NAFTA. *International Trade Journal* 15, 409 427.

Fama, E. F., (1965). The behavior of stock market prices. *Journal of Business* 38, 34-105.

Fang, W., (2001). Stock return process and expected depreciation over the Asian financial crisis. *Applied Economics* 33, 905-912.

Feenstra, R., & Taylor, A., (2008). *International trade*. New York: Worth Publishers.

Fiorentini, G., Sentana, E., & Calzolari, G., (2003). Maximum likelihood estimation and inference in multivariate conditionally heteroskedastic dynamic regression models with Student *t* innovations. *Journal of Business and Economic Statistics* 21, 532-546.

Fletcher, R., (1970). A new approach to variable metric algorithms. *Computer Journal* 13, 317-322.

Fraser, P., & Oyefeso, O., (2005). US, UK and European stock market integration. *Journal of Business Finance & Accounting* 32, 161-181.

Ghosh, A., Saidi, R., & Johnson, K. H., (1999). Who moves the Asia-Pacific stock markets-US or Japan? Empirical evidence based on the theory of cointegration. *Financial Review* 34, 159-170.

Gilmore, C. G., & McManus, G. M., (2004). The impact of NAFTA on the integration of the Canadian, Mexican, and U.S. equity markets. *Research in Global Strategic Management* 10, 137-151.

Globerman, S, & Shapiro, D., (1999). The impact of government policies on foreign direct investment: The Canadian experience. *Journal of International Business Studies* 30, 513-532.

Glosten, L., Jagannathan, R., & Runkle, D., (1993). Relationship between the expected values and the volatility of nominal excess returns on stocks. *Journal of Finance* 48, 1779-1801.

Goldfarb, D., (1970). A family of variable metric updates derived by variational means. *Mathematics of Computation* 24, 23-26.

Gonzalo, J., (1994). Five alternative methods of estimating long-run equilibrium relationships. *Journal of Econometrics* 60, 203-233.

Granger, C. W. J., (1986). Developments in the study of co-integrated economic variables. *Oxford Bulletin of Economics and Statistics* 48, 213-228.

Granger, C. W. J., (1992). Forecasting stock market prices: Lessons for forecasters. *International Journal of Forecasting* 8, 3-13.

Gregory, A., & Hansen, B.E., (1996). Residual–based tests for cointegration in models with regime shifts. *Journal of Econometrics* 70, 99-126.

Haas, M., Mittnik, S., & Paolella, M. S., (2006). Multivariate normal mixture GARCH. CFS Working Paper, No. 2006/09. Available at SSRN: http://ssrn.com/abstract=897461

Hahm, S-M., (2004). Transmission of stock returns and volatility: The case of Korea. *Journal of the Korean Economy* 5, 17-45.

Hamao, Y., Masulis, R., & Ng, V., (1990). Correlations in price changes and volatility across international stock markets. *The Review of Financial Studies* 3, 281-307.

Hannan, E. J., & Quinn, B. G., (1979) The determination of the order of an autoregression. *Journal of the Royal Statistical Society B* 41, 190-195.

Hansen, B.E., (1996). Inference when a nuisance parameter is not identified under the null hypothesis. *Econometrica* 64, 413-430.

Hansen, H., & Johansen, S., (1999). Some tests for parameter constancy in cointegrated VAR models. *Econometrics Journal* 2, 306-333.

Hansen, B., & Seo, B., (2002). Testing for two-regime threshold cointegration in vector error-correction models. *Journal of Econometrics* 110, 293-318.

Harvey, C., Ruiz, E., & Shephard, N., (1994). Multivariate stochastic variance models. *Review of Economic Studies* 61, 247-264.

Henry, O., (1998). Modelling the asymmetry of stock market volatility. *Applied Financial Economics* 8, 145-153.

Henry, O. T., & Sharma J. S., (1999). Asymmetric conditional volatility and firm size: evidence from Australian equity portfolios. *Australian Economic Papers* 38, 393-407.

Hjelm, G., & Johansson, M. W., (2005). A Monte Carlo study on the pitfalls in determining deterministic components in cointegrating models. *Journal of Macroeconomics*. 27, 691-703.

Hosking, J. R. M., (1980). The multivariate portmanteau statistic. *Journal of the American Statistical Association* 75, 602-608.

Hufbauer, G. C., & Schott, J. J., (2005). *NAFTA revisited.* Washington, DC: Institute for International Economics.

In, F., Kim, S., Yoon, J. H., & Viney, C., (2001). Dynamic interdependence and volatility transmission of Asian stock markets: Evidence from the Asian crisis. *International Review of Financial Analysis* 10, 87-96.

Jeon, B., & Chiang, T., (1991). A system of stock prices in world stock exchanges: Common stochastic trends for 1975-1990? *Journal of Economics and Business* 43, 329-338.

Jiang, C., & Chiang, T. C., (2000). Do foreign exchange risk premiums relate to the volatility in the foreign exchange and equity markets? *Applied Financial Economics* 10, 95-104.

Johansen, S., (1988). Statistical analysis of cointegration vectors. *Journal of Economic Dynamics and Control* 12, 231-254.

Johansen, S., (1991). Estimation and hypothesis testing of cointegration vectors in Gaussian vector autoregressive models. *Econometrica* 59, 1551-1580.

Johansen, S., (1995). *Likelihood-based inference in cointegrated vector autoregressive models.* New York: Oxford University Press.

Johansen, S., & Juselius, K., (1990). Maximum likelihood estimation and inference on cointegration with applications to demand for money. *Oxford Bulletin of Economics and Statistics* 52, 169-210.

Juselius, K., (2006). *The cointegrated VAR model: methodology and applications.* New York: Oxford University Press.

Kan, R., & Zhou, G., (2006). Modeling non-normality using multivariate t: Implications for asset pricing. Working Paper, University of Toronto and Washington University, St Louis.

Karolyi, G. A., (1995). A multivariate GARCH model of international transmissions of stock returns and volatility: The case of the United States and Canada. *Journal of Business and Economics Statistics* 13, 11-25.

Karp, N., & Sanchez, M., (2000). NAFTA's economic effects on Mexico. Economic Research Department, Mexico City. NBER 12th Annual Interamerican Seminar on Economics, Buenos Aires, December 2-4.

Kasa, K., (1992). Common stochastic trends in international stock markets. *Journal of Monetary Economics* 29, 95-124.

Kearney, C., & Patton, A. J., (2000). Multivariate GARCH modeling of exchange rate volatility transmission in the European Monetary System. *Financial Review* 35, 29-48.

Kearney, C., & Poti, V., (2006). Correlation dynamics in European equity markets. *Research in International Business and Finance* 20, 305-321.

King, M., & Wadhwani, S., (1990). Transmission of volatility between stock markets. *Review of Financial Studies* 3, 5-33.

Koop, G., Pesaran, M. H., & Potter, S. M., (1996). Impulse response analysis in nonlinear multivariate models. *Journal of Econometrics* 74, 119-147.

Koutmos, G., (1996). Modeling the dynamic interdependence of major European stock markets. *Journal of Business Finance & Accounting* 23, 975-988.

Koutmos, G., & Booth, G., (1995). Asymmetric volatility transmission in international stock markets. *Journal of International Money and Finance* 14, 747-762.

Kroner, K., & Ng, V., (1998). Modelling asymmetric comovements of asset returns. *Review of Financial Studies* 11, 817-844.

Kozubowski, T. J., & Podgorski, K., (2001). Asymmetric Laplace laws and modeling financial data. *Mathematical and Computer Modelling* 34, 1003-1021.

Kremers, J. J. M., Ericsson, N. R., & Dolado, J. J. , (1992). The power of cointegration tests. *Oxford Bulletin of Economics and Statistics* 54, 325-348.

Krugman, P., & Obstfeld, M., (2009). *International economics: Theory and policy*, 8th ed. Boston: Addison-Wesley.

Lee, B-S., & and Jeon, B. N., (1995). Common stochastic trends and predictability of international stock prices. *Journal of the Japanese and International Economics*. 9, 245-277.

Lin, W., Engle, R. F., & Ito, T., (1994). Do bulls and bears move across borders? International transmission of stock returns and volatility. *Review of Financial Studies* 7, 507-538.

Ling, S., & McAleer, M., (2003). Asymptotic theory for a vector ARMA-GARCH model. *Econometric Theory* 19, 278-308.

Liu, Y. A., Pan, M.-S., & Fung, H.-G., (1996). International transmission of stock price volatility: Evidence from the US and six Pacific Basin markets. *Journal of Multinational Financial Management* 6, 81-94.

Liu, Y. A., Pan, M.-S., & Shieh, J. C. P., (1998). International transmission of stock price movements: Evidence from the US and five Asian-Pacific markets. *Journal of Economics and Finance* 22, 59-69.

Lo, M. C., & E. Zivot, E., (2001). Threshold cointegration and nonlinear adjustment to the law of one price. *Macroeconomic Dynamics* 5, 533-576.

Lutkepohl H., (1991). *Introduction to multiple time series analysis.* Springer-Verlag, Berlin.

MacDermott, R., (2007). Regional trade agreement and foreign direct investment. *North American Journal of Economics and Finance* 18, 107-116.

MacKinnon, J. G., Haug, A. A., & Michelis, L., (1999). Numerical distribution functions of likelihood ratio tests for cointegration. *Journal of Applied Econometrics* 14, 563-577.

Manning, N., (2002). Common trends and convergence? South East Asian equity markets, 1988-1999. *Journal of International Money and Finance* 21, 183-202.

Masih, A. M. M., & Masih, R., (1997). Dynamic linkages and the propagation mechanism driving major international stock markets. *Quarterly Review of Economics and Finance* 37, 859-885.

Masih, A. M. M., & Masih, R., (2001). Long and short term dynamic causal transmission amongst international stock markets. *Journal of International Money and Finance* 20, 563-87.

McAleer, M., Chan, F., Hoti, S., & Lieberman, O., (2008). Generalized autoregressive conditional correlation. *Econometric Theory* 24, 1554-1583.

Mencía, F. J., & Sentana, E., (2004). Estimation and testing of dynamic models with generalised hyperbolic innovations. CEMFI working paper, No. 0411, Madrid, Spain.

Najand, M., & Yung, K., (1997). Price dynamics among exchange rates, stock index, and Treasury bonds in futures markets. *Advances in Investment Analysis and Portfolio Management* 4, 65-76.

Nelson, D. B., (1991). Conditional heteroskedasticity in asset returns: a new approach. *Econometrica* 59, 347-370.

Oehlert, G. W., (1992). A note on the delta method. *American Statistician* 46, 27-29.

Ortiz, E., López Herrera, F., & Cabello, A., (2008). Returns and volatility dynamics from the NAFTA stock markets. The Business Association of Latin American Studies, Annual Conference, Bogota, Columbia, April.

Ostermark, R., (2001). Multivariate cointegration analysis of the Finnish-Japanese stock markets. *European Journal of Operational Research* 134, 498-507.

Osterwald-Lenum, M., (1992). A note with quantiles of the asymptotic distribution of the maximum likelihood cointegration rank tests statistics. *Oxford Bulletin of Economics and Statistics* 54, 461-472.

Pagan, A. R., & Schwert, G. W., (1990). Alternative models for conditional stock volatility. *Journal of Econometrics* 45, 267-290.

Pan, M. S., Liu, Y. A., & Roth, H. J., (1999). Common stochastic trends and volatility in Asian-Pacific equity markets. *Global Finance Journal* 10, 161-172.

Pascual, A.G., (2003). Assessing European stock markets cointegration. *Economics Letters* 78, 197-203.

Perron, P., (1989).The Great Crash, the oil shock and the unit root hypothesis. *Econometrica* 57, 1361-1402.

Pesaran, M. H., & Shin, Y., (1998). Generalized impulse response analysis in linear multivariate models. *Economic Letters* 58, 17-29.

Phengpis, C., & Swanson, P., (2006). Portfolio diversification effects of trading blocs: The case of NAFTA. *Journal of Multinational Financial Management* 16, 315-331.

Phillips, P. C. B., & Perron, P., (1988). Testing for a unit root in time series regressions. *Biometrika* 75, 335-346.

Ploberger, W., Kramer, W., & Kontrus, K., (1989). A new test for structural stability in the linear regression model. *Journal of Econometrics* 40, 307-318

Poterba, J. M., & Summers, L. H., (1986). The persistence of volatility and stock market fluctuations. *American Economic Review* 76, 1142-1151.

Rahbek, A., Hansen, E., & Dennis, J., (2002). ARCH innovations and their impact on cointegration rank testing. Department of Statistics, University of Copenhagen, Working Paper, 22, 2002, Copenhagen.

Rangvid, J., (2001). Increasing convergence among European stock markets? A recursive common stochastic trends analysis. *Economic Letters* 71, 383-389.

Rangvid, J., & Sorensen, C., (2002). Convergence in the ERM and declining numbers of common stochastic trends. *Journal of Emerging Market Finance* 1, 183-213.

Richards, A. J., (1995). Comovements in national stock market returns: evidence of predictability, but not cointegration. *Journal of Monetary Economics* 36, 631-654.

Roca, E. D., (1999). Short-term and long-term price linkages between the equity markets of Australia and its major trading partners. *Applied Financial Economics* 9, 501-511.

Sen, A., (2003). On unit root tests when the alternative is a trend break stationary process. *Journal of Business and Economic Statistics* 21, 174-184.

Sentana, E., (1995). Quadratic ARCH models. *Review of Economic Studies* 62, 639-661.

Shanno, D. F., (1970). Conditioning of quasi-Newton methods for function minimization. *Mathematics of Computation* 24, 647-656.

Sharma, S. C., & Wongbangpo, P., (2002). Long-term trends and cycles in ASEAN stock markets. *Review of Financial Economics* 11, 299-315.

Shenton, L. R., & Bowman, K. O., (1977). A bivariate model for the distribution of $\sqrt{b_1}$ and b_2. *Journal of the American Statistical Association* 72, 206-211.

Sims, C. A., (1980). Macroeconomics and reality. *Econometrica* 48, 1-48.

Schwarz, G., (1978).Estimating the dimension of a model. *Annals of Statistics* 6, 461-464.

Taylor, M. P., & Tonks, I., (1989). The internationalisation of stock markets and the abolition of U.K. exchange control. *Review of Economics and Statistics* 71, 332-336.

Theodosiou, P., & Lee, U., (1993). Mean and volatility spillovers across major national markets: Further empirical evidence. *Journal of Financial Research* 16, 337-350.

Tsay, R. S., (1989). Testing and modeling threshold autoregressive processes. *Journal of the American Statistical Association* 84, 231-240.

Tse, Y. K., & Tsui, A. K. C., (2002). A multivariate GARCH model with time-varying correlations. *Journal of Business and Economic Statistics* 20, 351-362.

Vlaar, P., & Palm, F., (1993). The message in weekly exchange rates in the European Monetary System: Mean reversion, conditional heteroskedasticity, and jumps. *Journal of Business and Economic Statistics* 11, 351-360.

Wang, P., Liu, A., & Wang, P., (2004). Return and risk interactions in Chinese stock markets. *Journal of International Financial Markets, Institutions & Money* 14, 367-384.

Wilson, E., & Hilferty, M., (1931). The distribution of chi-square. *Proceedings National Academy of Sciences* 17, 684-688.

Worthington, A., & Higgs, H., (2004). Transmission of equity returns and volatility in Asian developed and emerging markets: a multivariate GARCH analysis. *International Journal of Finance & Economics* 9, 71-80.

Yang, J., Kolari, J. W., & Min, I., (2003). Stock market integration and financial crises: the case of Asia. *Applied Financial Economics* 13, 477–86.

Zakoian, J. M., (1994). Threshold heteroskedastic models. *Journal of Economic Dynamics and Control* 18, 931-935.

Zivot, E., & Andrews, D. W. K., (1992). Further evidence on the great crash, the oil-price shock and the unit root hypothesis. *Journal of Business and Economic Statistics* 10, 251-270.

INDEX

A

B

C

F

G

H

I

N

O

P

R

S

T

U

V

W

Y